A–Z

OF

SHEFFIELD

PLACES - PEOPLE - HISTORY

Melvyn and Joan Jones

AMBERLEY

First published 2019

Amberley Publishing
The Hill, Stroud, Gloucestershire, GL5 4EP
www.amberley-books.com

Copyright © Melvyn and Joan Jones, 2019

The right of Melvyn and Joan Jones to be
identified as the Authors of this work has been
asserted in accordance with the Copyrights,
Designs and Patents Act 1988.

ISBN 978 1 4456 8183 2 (print)
ISBN 978 1 4456 8184 9 (ebook)

British Library Cataloguing in Publication Data.
A catalogue record for this book is available
from the British Library.

Origination by Amberley Publishing.
Printed in Great Britain.

Contents

Introduction

Selecting the contents of this book has been very difficult. At least two or three books could be written on Sheffield in this format. And we say that having included two or three places for twelve of the letters of the alphabet in this volume.

There was a wealth of material from almost every period: Prehistoric, Dark Ages, Middle Ages, Tudor, Elizabethan, Georgian, Victorian and on to the late twentieth century and beyond. There is the industrial heritage (including industrial museums), historic buildings from the medieval period to the early twentieth century and, of course, stunning parks, gardens and the countryside. Oh the countryside! There are the rivers that flow down rural and semi-rural valleys from the moorland edge to the centre of the city, the Pennine moorlands and upland farming areas (including 29,000 acres within the Peak District National Park), the city's own lake district (i.e. reservoirs in the upland valleys), and ancient woodlands galore. Although the city is still a major centre of specialist steel production, it is now not only known as 'Steel City' but also as the greenest city in the country.

And these places are strongly associated with notable people including Robin Hood; Mary, Queen of Scots; the Earls of Shrewsbury; Dukes of Norfolk; Admiral Nelson's chaplain and secret agent Alexander John Scott; the sculptor Sir Francis Chantrey; the 'Corn Law Rhymer' Ebenezer Elliott; and the inventor of stainless steel, Harry Brearley.

Altogether the places and people described ought to make Sheffielders proud of their heritage and visitors surprised and a little envious! So read on. Going through the alphabet really does open the doorway to history and heritage.

A

Abbeydale Industrial Hamlet

Abbeydale Industrial Hamlet is just that. It comprises a beautifully preserved old scythe works where the crucible steel was made, scythes shaped and finally their cutting edges ground. There is also a furnished manager's house, a counting house, workmen's cottages and stables. The last tenant, Tyzack, Sons & Turner, who had tenanted the site since 1849, quit the works in 1933. It was purchased in 1935 by the philanthropist Alderman J. G. Graves, and presented to the city to be used as a museum, but it did not open as a museum until 1970. The City Council closed the museum in 1997. It was then leased to the Sheffield Industrial Museums Trust, who reopened it the following year.

Above: Tilt hammers at Abbeydale Industrial Hamlet. (Courtesy of Sheffield Industrial Museums Trust)

Right: The upper level of a set of crucible furnaces at Abbeydale Industrial Hamlet. (Courtesy of Sheffield Industrial Museums Trust)

The grinding hull at Abbeydale Industrial Hamlet. (Courtesy of Sheffield Industrial Museums Trust)

The early industrial history of the site is uncertain. There is circumstantial evidence that it may well have been in existence as early as the late sixteenth century as a lead-smelting mill but it was certainly in existence by the late seventeenth century, possibly as a cutler's wheel. At that time water from the River Sheaf entered the works to drive a waterwheel via an artificially made channel called a goit, but later the reservoir or 'dam', as such creations are known locally, was made and enlarged to provide the water power for several waterwheels, and the dam survives to this day. At first the steel for the scythe making would have been brought from furnaces elsewhere but in the 1770s crucible steel making was introduced to the site and it became a fully integrated scythe-making enterprise. The crucible steel furnace can be investigated at close quarters: the lower level where the crucibles full of blister steel were heated in coke-filled furnaces for three hours and the upper level where the puller out and the teemer worked to pour the molten steel into moulds. The crucible furnace still has the characteristic tall brick chimney stack. Next door is a tilt hammer where the blades were shaped and nearby are the grinding hulls where the blades were ground.

B

Beauchief Abbey, Botanical Gardens and Bradfield Village

Beauchief Abbey was formerly in the part of north Derbyshire that became part of Sheffield at the beginning of the twentieth century. The name Beauchief is Norman-French and means 'beautiful headland'. And that is exactly what the site looks like, a wooded headland, when viewed from the edge of the moors to the south-west. It is pronounced 'Bee-chif'. The abbey was founded between 1173 and 1176 by Robert Fitzranulf, lord of the manor of Norton and Alfreton, for the Premonstratensians, who were known as the White Canons and were noted for founding their monastic houses in isolated locations and living in poverty. The neighbouring suburbs of Abbeydale and Millhouses get their names from the presence of the abbey and its water-powered mills. In return for the generous grants of land by the neighbouring lord of the manor, the canons gave daily services at his chapel at Ecclesall. When the abbey was dissolved in 1537 the tower of the abbey church was converted into a private chapel for the new owner and religious services still take place there.

Situated less than a mile from Sheffield city centre, the **Botanical Gardens** consist of 19 acres of gardens with a wonderful variety of trees from around the world in fifteen 'character areas', formal bedding displays, the restored Grade II* glasshouses and even a bear pit. It all began in 1833 when Sheffield Botanical and Horticultural Society was formed to develop a botanical garden. A national competition was held to design the gardens, glass pavilions, entrances and lodges. One of the judges was Joseph Paxton of Chatsworth and Crystal Palace fame. Robert Marnock, the gardener at Bretton Hall in West Yorkshire, won the competition and Benjamin Broomhead Taylor, a Sheffield architect, was awarded second prize. Robert Marnock was appointed head gardener and he laid out the gardens in the then highly fashionable 'gardenesque' style where each plant was displayed to perfection in scattered plantings. The glass pavilions are thought to be the result of collaboration between Marnock, Taylor, Paxton and John Loudon. The resulting structure is almost 100 metres long. The grand entrance to the gardens on Clarkehouse Road was designed by Taylor.

Left: Beauchief Abbey.

Below: The restored pavilions at Sheffield Botanical Gardens.

The gardens were opened to the public on 29 and 30 of June and 4 and 5 July 1833 – by ticket only. Around 12, 000 people visited on the opening days. But between 1836 and 1898 entry was limited to shareholders and annual subscribers except for special fêtes and galas when entry was still sufficiently expensive to exclude the majority of the local population. The gardens sank into debt in 1897 and were taken over by the Town Trust, who instituted free entrance for all. The City Council took over management in 1951. In the last two decades of the twentieth century financial restrictions resulted in neglect. The glass pavilions were closed to the public from the late 1990s having become dilapidated.

In 1997 a partnership between The Friends of the Botanical Gardens (formed in 1984), the Town Trust, the City Council and the University of Sheffield made a bid to the Heritage Lottery Fund for complete restoration of the entire gardens, buildings and plantings. An award of just over £5 million was made in May 1997. As a result, and after further fundraising, the gardens were transformed and the pavilions and gatehouse restored to their former splendour. The Curator's House is now a restaurant and tearoom and the Dorothy Fox Education Centre was opened in the gardens in 2017. They are gardens to be proud of again.

At **Bradfield** there are in fact two villages: Low Bradfield and High Bradfield. Dominating High Bradfield is St Nicholas' Parish Church. The oldest part of this large church is the clock/bell tower dating from around 1475. The views from the

Looking across the flower beds towards the gateway lodge at Sheffield Botanical Gardens.

churchyard over the surrounding countryside are glorious. One has to pinch oneself to remember that the centre of a city containing more than half a million people lies just over 6 miles to the south-east.

The churchyard contains some very old gravestones including one particularly interesting one dating from 1864 when the nearby Dale Dyke Reservoir burst its banks and the torrent of water, rushing down the Loxley valley towards Sheffield, resulted in the death of 240 people. The gravestone in question is that of James Trickett, his wife and three children who all perished in the flood. The last two lines of the dedication read, 'Whate'er the fault this is most true, The Flood is a warning to me and to you'. At the entrance to the churchyard is what is reputed to have been a watch-house built around 1830 as a lookout point to discourage bodysnatchers disinterring newly buried bodies.

To the west of the church, on what is significantly called Bailey Hill, are the earthworks of a motte-and-bailey castle. The motte (the mound that was the lookout site and might have had a timber-framed building at its top) is 60 feet high and surrounded by a deep ditch. The bailey covers three-quarters of an acre and is also surrounded by a bank and ditch. This archaeological feature is best visited in winter when the trees that have colonised the site have shed their leaves.

St Nicholas' Church, Bradfield.

Above: View over the upper Loxley valley from the doorway of St Nicholas' Church, Bradfield.

Right: The gravestone of the Trickett family.

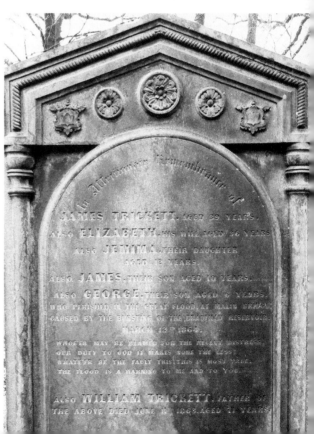

In Affectionate Remembrance of
JAMES TRICKETT, AGED 39 YEARS.
ALSO ELIZABETH, HIS WIFE AGED 36 YEARS
ALSO JEMIMA, THEIR DAUGHTER
AGED 12 YEARS.
ALSO JAMES, THEIR SON AGED 10 YEARS.
ALSO GEORGE, THEIR SON AGED 6 YEARS.
WHO PERISHED IN THE GREAT FLOOD, AT MALIN BRIDGE,
CAUSED BY THE BURSTING OF THE BRADFIELD RESERVOIR.
MARCH 12TH 1864.

WHOEVER MAY BE BLAMED FOR THE RECENT DISTRESS,
OUR DUTY TO GOD IT MAKES NONE THE LESS,
WHATEVER BE THE FAULT THIS—THIS IS MOST TRUE,
THE FLOOD IS A WARNING TO ME AND TO YOU.

ALSO WILLIAM TRICKETT, FATHER OF
THE ABOVE DIED JUNE 1st 1865 AGED 71 YEARS

Cementation Furnace, Cholera Monument and the Cutlers' Hall

Until the second half of the eighteenth century the steel used by Sheffield's cutlers was either imported or was locally made 'shear steel', which was forged from 'blister steel' made in a cementation furnace. Some 260 such furnaces, easily recognised by their conical shape, were eventually built in the Sheffield area of which only one remains standing, on Doncaster Street. It was probably built between 1830 and 1840 and was once part of the Daniel Doncaster works. It last worked in 1951.

In a cementation furnace in two sandstone chests were put alternate layers of charcoal and iron bars covered by a layer of mortar made from 'wheelswarf' – the

The cementation furnace, Doncaster Street.

debris of sand and steel grindings from the bottom of a grinder's trough. The furnace was sealed and a coal fire lit below the sandstone chests, which burned for seven to nine days. After around a week of cooling down the furnace was opened and the iron bars now converted to blister steel (they were covered in small blisters) were removed. Incidentally, the hard crust from the top of the chests, called 'crozzle', can still be seen topping walls throughout the Sheffield area. The bars of blister steel were then converted into shear steel by being heated in bundles to bright red and then forged into a uniform bar. Shear steel could be ground to produce a sharp cutting edge but was still not completely uniform in carbon content and therefore uniformity and was not suitable for all steel products.

The **Cholera Monument** commemorates one of Sheffield's greatest disasters. The problems of overcrowding and a deficient public water supply led to the deaths of 402 inhabitants of Sheffield in 1832 from a violent outbreak of the disease. The town's population grew very sharply in the early nineteenth century. In 1801 the population had grown to nearly 46,000 and by the time of the 1831 census it had soared to more than 90,000. Although the population growth had been accompanied by substantial housing expansion, the town was still a very crowded place with many of its poorest inhabitants living in back-to-back housing built around small yards or 'courts', a considerable proportion of them still obtaining their drinking water from wells. Even where piped water was available it was often obtained from a standpipe in the yard. There was a constant danger of leakage from the shared privies and primitive drains into the drinking supply.

The cholera bacillus must be swallowed to take effect. It is swallowed when drinking contaminated water and is particularly rife where the water supply is polluted. Cholera is not contagious, although this is what was thought in the early nineteenth century. The upper floors of Kelham Island Workhouse were used as a cholera isolation hospital in Sheffield in 1832 but inevitably this did not stop the disease from spreading.

The disease entered Britain at Sunderland on 19 October 1831. By the time it had run its course in the British Isles, 25,000 men, women and children had died in Ireland, 9,500 in Scotland and 22,000 in England. The first confirmed case appeared in Sheffield on 8 July 1832. The disease raged through the town throughout July, August and September, but by the beginning of October the worst was over and only one case was reported after 8 December. After 8 August burials in public graveyards were forbidden and from then on they took place in a special burial ground in Norfolk Road where in 1834 the Cholera Monument was erected.

The **Cutlers' Hall**, headquarters of the Company of Cutlers in Hallamshire, which came into being in 1624, stands on Church Street opposite the cathedral. The present hall, in Grecian style with four Corinthian columns, was the third hall to be built for the Cutlers and was completed in 1832 and extended in 1888. The interior is magnificent. It is a Grade II* listed building.

The Company of Cutlers was founded as a result of a bill passed by the House of Commons in April 1624 'for the Good Order and Government of the Makers of Knives,

The Cholera Monument.

Sickles, Shears, Scissors and other Cutlery Wares in Hallamshire...'. The Cutlers' Company was responsible for regulating apprenticeships and issuing marks. One of its important recent roles is the protection of trademarks. At the time of its foundation there were 498 master craftsmen in Hallamshire and by 1682 the number had risen to 2,000. The Cutlers' Hall contains the company's archives, an outstanding collection of paintings and sculptures and a stunning collection of cutlery and silverware, including examples of the famous Bowie knife that was made by a number of Sheffield cutlery firms.

Banqueting suite in the Cutlers' Hall. (Courtesy of the Company of Cutlers in Hallamshire)

A display of silverware in the Cutlers' Hall. (Courtesy of the Company of Cutlers in Hallamshire)

Dale Dyke Reservoir and Dore Village

Dale Dyke (or Dike) Reservoir (or Dam as it is more familiarly known) lies in the upper Loxley valley just 8 miles from the centre of Sheffield. And if you partake in the signposted walk around the reservoir surrounded by woodland and hill pasture it is difficult to realise that this was at the heart of one of the worst disasters in Britain. Just before midnight on 11 March 1864, after several days of heavy rain in this peaceful valley, the original Dale Dyke Reservoir, built between 1859 and 1864 by the Sheffield Waterworks Company, collapsed and the waters burst down the valley towards Sheffield.

A view looking down to the Dale Dyke Dam.

The message that a crack had been found in the embankment holding back the newly built reservoir's waters was delivered by Stephenson Fountain, the son of one of the subcontractors on the site, to John Gunson, the chief engineer, in his home in Sheffield just before eight o'clock in the evening. Gunson then set off in his gig to investigate and arrived at the dam around ten o'clock. Despite attempts to relieve the pressure on the embankment wall by opening the valves to allow water to escape and blowing a hole with dynamite in part of the wall, the dam wall burst open and millions of gallons of water began their destructive journey down the Loxley valley. Little warning could be given. Altogether it is estimated that 600 million gallons of water surged down the valley. It was the dead of night and the only travel possible was either on foot or by horsepower.

The crushing torrent of water swept everything before it – cottages, farm buildings, water-powered mills, bridges, farm livestock and people. The waters swept on, unstoppable, into central Sheffield along the River Don and on to Rotherham and Mexbrough and even Doncaster where the next morning there was still enough water to flood cellars. Two hundred and forty people were drowned, 415 houses and 106 works and shops were completely or partially destroyed, 693 farm animals were lost and fifteen stone bridges were swept away. One human body was found on the outskirts of Doncaster.

The once Derbyshire village of **Dore** (it was transferred from Derbyshire in 1935) is one of the most desirable suburbs of Sheffield. Christ Church was built in

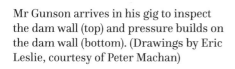

Mr Gunson arrives in his gig to inspect the dam wall (top) and pressure builds on the dam wall (bottom). (Drawings by Eric Leslie, courtesy of Peter Machan)

1829 and became the parish church in 1844 after Dore became a separate parish, rather than a township in a large north Derbyshire parish. The public house name *The Devonshire Arms* reflects the fact that the Duke of Devonshire's Derbyshire properties extended as far north as the outskirts of Sheffield. The place name Dore is an Old English name and literally means a door or narrow passage, in this case between the two Anglo-Saxon kingdoms of Mercia to the south and Northumbria to the north. The Limb Brook, which forms the northern boundary of Dore, runs down from Whirlow (which means boundary mound) and flows into the River Sheaf, the river name also meaning boundary. This boundary was also between Derbyshire and Yorkshire and the boundary between the seas of the Archbishop of Canterbury and the Archbishop of York. A plaque erected on the village green in 1968 by the Dore Village Society commemorates a historic meeting that took place in the village in 829. In that year King Egbert of Wessex came to Dore to accept the submission of King Eanred of Northumbria, thus uniting Anglo-Saxon Britain under one king. The Anglo-Saxon Chronicle also records that in 942 Edmund, the son of Edward the Elder, had conquered the Danes of Mercia 'as far as Dore divides'.

Plaque on Dore village green.

E

Ecclesall Woods and Ecclesfield Church, Churchyard and Priory

Ecclesall Woods are not only a popular recreation space and a valuable wildlife habitat, but also an important historical monument and industrial archaeological site. And it is Ecclesall Woods not Ecclesall Wood because in the past the woodland block was made up of many separate woods each with its own name. In the seventeenth century it was made up of twenty-three woods including Snaithing Spring, which is the only one that is separate from the main block of woodland.

The woods were part of the manor of Ecclesall in the Middle Ages and descended with the manor from the de Ecclesall family through a number of other owners before being acquired in the seventeenth century by the Bright family. The woods remained with the Bright family until 1752 when the Bright heiress, Mary Bright, married the 2nd Marquis of Rockingham of Wentworth Woodhouse. On the death of the 2nd Marquis in 1782 they passed to the Earls Fitzwilliam, from whom they were purchased by Sheffield Corporation in 1927.

In 1319 Sir Robert de Ecclesall was granted a licence to create a deer park around his manor house in Ecclesall. Such parks were not primarily for hunting deer but were status symbols and to ensure a reliable supply of venison, rabbit and fish (from fish ponds) for the table and wood and timber from the woods within the park. There is substantial place name evidence to suggest that the present Ecclesall Woods were incorporated into the park: the area at the northern end of the woods is still called Park Head, and there used to be two fields to the east of the woods called Old Park and Park Field.

By the sixteenth century the site had been converted into a large area of woodland that was managed as coppice-with-standards woods until well into the nineteenth century. The wood (cut from the coppice stools) and the timber (from the single-stemmed standard trees) had a remarkable number of uses. Nothing was wasted. Even the smallest brushwood and twigs were bundled up to make faggots to heat bakers' ovens, to make besoms and to protect the goits (artificial waterways that led water from the river to the dam and then from the dam back to the river at the many water-powered industrial sites). By the second half of the nineteenth century, like most local woods Ecclesall Woods was converted into canopy woods to produce timber from single-stemmed trees.

Bluebells around an oak tree in Ecclesall Woods.

Since the site was officially opened by the Princess Royal in 1928, Ecclesall Woods has been managed as a public recreational space. Recent management has included thinning operations, glade creation and footpath improvements. These have been accompanied by interpretive initiatives by the very active Friends of Ecclesall Woods group. An exciting development in the last few years has been the taking back into City Council control of Ecclesall Woods Sawmill site and the erection of a woodland gallery (Hector's House) that was opened in 2008 and the J. G. Graves Discovery Centre opened in 2011. Craft courses are offered throughout the year and exciting spaces can be hired for parties and weddings.

Because of their great size (320 acres) and their changing use over the centuries, and the great variety of habitats within them, Ecclesall Woods constitute not only a diverse natural environment, including a bird sanctuary, but are also a treasure house of archaeology. The archaeology includes archaeology *of the woods* (for example, whitecoal kilns, charcoal-making sites and even a monument to a charcoal maker) and archaeology *in the woods*, that is, archaeology that happens to have been preserved within a woodland environment but has nothing specifically to do with the woodland environment, for example, quarrying and mining sites, the site of a prehistoric hilltop enclosure and prehistoric 'cup and ring' marked stones. The most unusual sites of archaeology of the woods are circular hollows, known as whitecoal kilns or Q-pits. In a whitecoal kiln slivers of wood were dried over a fire to drive out the moisture. Whitecoal was used as a fuel in lead smelting at local water-powered sites between 1575 and 1750. There are at least 150 whitecoal kilns in Ecclesall Woods. The wood is now bisected by Abbey Lane. Around halfway up the lane if you cross the road and walk into the northern part of the wood you will see the monument to the wood collier (i.e. charcoal maker) George Yardley, who was burnt to death here in 1786. Immediately to the left of the monument is a levelled area thought to be the site of a charcoal hearth where coppice poles were converted into charcoal. There are around 300 charcoal hearths in Ecclesall Woods.

Above left: The J. G. Graves Discovery Centre, Ecclesall Woods.

Above right: George Yardley's monument , Ecclesall Woods.

St Mary's Church, Ecclesfield, was once known as the 'minster of the moors' because of the very large parish that it served, covering 50,000 acres or 78 square miles. A church has stood on the site since at least the early twelfth century but the present church is largely the result of rebuilding at the end of the fifteenth century in the Perpendicular style. Important internal changes took place in the nineteenth century. The church contains interesting monuments and stained-glass windows. The most eye-catching monument is the one to Sir Richard Scott who died in 1638. He lies on his side in his armour with his left hand resting on his cheek. He was Comptroller of the household of Thomas Wentworth, 1st Earl of Strafford, and his deputy when Strafford was Lord Deputy of Ireland. On the northern wall of the nave are the colours of the Ecclesfield Volunteers who were raised in 1803 to defend the country against Napoleon. There are also six of their swords and three of their bugles. Apart from one window on the north wall of the nave, which is made up of fragments of medieval windows, all the windows are Victorian. These include one window on the south wall of the nave dedicated to Margaret Gatty, wife of Alfred Gatty who was vicar from 1839 until 1903. Mrs Gatty was a renowned children's writer and pioneering marine biologist. The bottom part of the window celebrates her series of books called

Above: St Mary's Church, Ecclesfield.

Left: Interior of Ecclesfield church showing the Sir Richard Scott monument in a painting by Margaret Scott Gatty. (Courtesy of Sheffield City Archives)

Parables from Nature and depicts the parables of the Sower, the Sparrows, the Barren Fig Tree, the Lost Sheep and Sorting the Fishes. Another window on the north wall of the nave is dedicated to Dr and Mrs Gatty's daughter, Juliana Ewing, who was even more famous than her mother as a children's writer. All but one of the angels have long flowing hair. The exception has hers in a chignon, a hairstyle always associated with Juliana.

Ecclesfield churchyard is also full of interest. It contains the graves of Alfred and Margaret Gatty, and in the same grave is buried Mrs Gatty's father, the Revd Alexander John Scott. Scott, a brilliant linguist, was Admiral Nelson's chaplain and secret agent, and Nelson died in his arms at the Battle of Trafalgar. Also buried in the churchyard are Joseph Hunter, Sheffield's first local historian, author of the monumental *History and Topography of Hallamshire* and the first book ever published on the West Riding dialect, and Parkin Jeffcock, the mining engineer who lost his life in the explosion at the Oaks Colliery in 1866 when 361 men and boys were killed.

Just outside the churchyard is **Ecclesfield Priory**. It was built to accommodate the monks of the Benedictine abbey of St Wandrille in Normandy who had been granted the church and surrounding land in the parish of Ecclesfield by the lord of the manor of Hallamshire, Richard de Lovetot, in the twelfth century. The first mention of the priory was in 1273. Unlike most medieval priories that are in ruins, Ecclesfield Priory was converted into a private house, which it remains to this day.

The gravestone of Alexander John Scott, Admiral Nelson's chaplain and secret agent.

Firth Park, Fitzalan Square and Fulwood Old Chapel

Firth Park was Sheffield's first publicly owned park, donated to the then town by steel manufacturer Mark Firth. The opening ceremony took place on 16 August 1875 when Mark Firth was Mayor of Sheffield. It was opened by Edward, Prince of Wales, the future King Edward VII, and his wife Princess Alexandra. And what an occasion! The royal couple went from the Victoria railway station, which had been transformed

The opening of Firth Park, 16 August 1875. (*The Graphic*, 21 August 1875)

into a huge conservatory, by carriage drawn by four magnificent horses in a long procession led by the band of the 7th Hussars. The route was lined by cheering crowds and adorned with flowers and bunting. There were flags flying from every house top, church steeple and factory roof.

When the royal party arrived at the entrance to the park a salute was fired by a military battery and the prince and princess took their seats in a 'grand pavilion' crowned by 'a large Turkish minaret'. Directly opposite the pavilion were 15,000 Sunday school scholars who sang the national anthem accompanied by military bands. The Archbishop of York said a prayer, Mark Firth handed over to the prince the deeds of the park, in which he dedicated it 'for ever to the public use and enjoyment of the people'. The prince in his turn presented them to the town clerk declaring the park to be opened.

For almost the next 100 years every part of the 36-acre park flourished and was heavily used. The park is made up of a long spur of land flanked by two valleys each containing a small stream. The promontory had paths for 'promenading' and areas for formal (cricket and football) and informal games. The two valleys were (and remain) wooded. Brushes Wood, in the east, is an ancient oak wood mentioned in 1637 as a spring (coppice) wood. In 1909 Hinde Common Wood, to the south of Brushes Wood, was purchased and added to the park. The main entrance to the park was at the Clock Tower, the focal point of the park in its early days. It incorporated the park keeper's house, rooms for refreshment, and a veranda where visitors could shelter in inclement weather.

One organisation that has stood the test of time is Firth Park Bowling Club, one of the founder members of Sheffield & District Crown Green Bowling Association, which was founded in 1908. In 1949 a new entrance layout to Firth Park was approved near the present roundabout. The 1950s saw a rose garden established near the North Lodge and in the 1960s the duck pond was often used for model ship regattas. In the 1970s a children's playground was constructed near Hucklow Road.

In 2000 a Friends of Firth Park group was formed and is involved in practical work and fundraising. A new £100,000 playground was opened in April 2004, with two sections: one for those under the age of five and another for five- to twelve-year-olds. Sheffield was a successful applicant in the government's national design competition for improving and extending nursery provision. The new nursery, at the top of the park, costing £1.8m, was opened in 2005. Besides its space for pre-school children it has office space, a café, a meeting room, exhibition space, public toilets, a ranger base, and an underground store for park maintenance equipment.

Fitzalan Square, so called after one of the family names of the Dukes of Norfolk, the major private landowner in Sheffield, was laid out over a protracted period from 1869 to 1881. Early twentieth-century photographs of the square show it as an important tram terminus and crowded with waiting horse cabs. At the centre of the square is a bronze statue of King Edward VII dating from 1913 by Alfred Drury. On the pedestal are depicted scenes representing Philanthropy, Peace and Unity. The Philanthropy

A view of Firth Park today.

scene shows human figures holding aloft a model of the King Edward VII Hospital. Around the square there are two interesting buildings: the former General Post Office and the White Building. The former General Post Office was erected in 1910 from sandstone quarried at Grenoside. It closed in 1999 and following a £9m regeneration project it reopened in 2016 as the home of the Institute of Arts of Sheffield Hallam University. The White Building lies on the western side of Fitzalan Square, its name gained from the white faience covering to its walls. Four storeys high and, unusually for Sheffield, with balconied windows on the first and third floors, it is the reliefs at first-floor level, above the shops, that occupy the ground floor, that draw the eye. There are ten altogether showing Sheffield trades and were created by the Tory family in 1908.

Fulwood Old Chapel on Whiteley Lane, Fulwood, a Unitarian place of worship, is simple but appealing and dates from 1728. It is Grade II listed. Money to build 'a large and handsome Chapel' was left in the will of Fulwood resident William Ronksley. It has an adjoining schoolroom and at the rear is the old Chapel House where the minister once resided. Samuel Plimsoll (1824–98), who through parliament in 1875 introduced 'The Plimsoll Line' on ships, worshipped here when he lived at Whiteley Wood Hall. The Plimsoll Line indicated the maximum depth to which a ship may

Above: Two reliefs on the White Building in Fitzalan Square: left, a buffer and right, a cutler.

Right: A relief of an engineer on the White Building in Fitzalan Square.

Fulwood Old Chapel.

be safely immersed when loaded with cargo. In 1930 the Plimsoll Line was adopted by fifty-four maritime nations. One of Plimsoll's daughters is said to be buried at the chapel.

In the chapel garden are the old village stocks, moved there from the village green when road widening took place. Stocks were an ancient form of punishment for petty criminals. They were ridiculed by having their feet (and sometimes their hands) locked in a wooden structure fixed into upright stone or wooden posts. The stocks were located on the village green or market place in full view of the public where petty criminals could be jeered at. The practice only ceased in the middle of the nineteenth century.

G

Grenoside

For many centuries the villagers of Grenoside and those living in the surrounding countryside inhabited a woodland world. The village was (and still is) surrounded on the north and west by extensive ancient woodlands. Local place names indicate early settlement in an almost completely wooded environment, and many village occupations were once directly or indirectly connected with timber and wood. Today Birkin Royd, Prior Royd and Wheata Wood are amenity woods owned by the City Council and Greno Wood and Hall Wood are owned and managed by Sheffield and Rotherham Wildlife Trust.

The name of the village, which was first recorded in the thirteenth century as *Gravenhou*, is made up of three elements: Gren (from the Old English *grefen*), o (from the Old Norse *haugr*) and side, altogether meaning quarried-hill-side. The village lies on the dip slope of a westward-facing sandstone escarpment at between 175 m (575 ft) and 245 m (800 ft). The sandstone, the outcrop of which forms Jawbone Hill to the west of the village, is the Grenoside sandstone. This sandstone was once extensively quarried to produce ashlar blocks and grindstones. Hillsborough Barracks (now Morrison's superstore) and the old Post Office building in Fitzalan Square are reputed to be of Grenoside sandstone.

From Main Street it is interesting to scan the horizon to the east. There are views towards Wentworth church, Hoober Stand and Keppel's Column in the middle distance. On the horizon on a clear day the cooling towers of Drax power station can also be seen. A visitor to the area in 1639 said he could see Lincoln Cathedral and York Minster. But then he also called the heights above Grenoside and Wortley 'cloud kissed mountains'! At the top of Norfolk Hill stands the Old Harrow public house. It is here every Boxing Day morning that the Grenoside Sword Dancers perform their age-old dance.

An interesting part of the village lies up Bower Lane, on Middle Lane, Stephen Lane and Top Side. In this part of Grenoside there are still many stone-built cottages with their assorted outhouses, occasional farmhouses and stone-walled cottage gardens, all helping to impart a village atmosphere. The introduction to a story by the Ecclesfield-born children's writer Juliana Ewing (1841–85), *Mrs Overtheway's Remembrances*,

Above: Old Harrow public house, Grenoside.

Below: Old water trough, Grenoside.

is set in this part of the village and she specifically mentions the stone water troughs that are still found here. Near the lower of the two stone troughs in Bower Lane is the old stone-walled village pinfold where stray animals were once impounded. A fine had to be paid before they were released.

A walk in Greno Wood is full of interest. On the left of the track not far into the southern entrance to the wood visitors should look for a small pond among the trees. This is Sharpe's 'wood 'oyl' where the Sharpes obtained their water supply for basket-making. In the 1881 census William Sharpe, basket-maker, lived in Lump Lane, Grenoside, and employed three men. They specialised in making 'swill' or 'spelk' baskets, which were made from lengths of thinly split oak. The oak was boiled to make it easier to split and weave.

Other unusual sights in the wood are ant nests and carpets of common cow-wheat. The wood ant nests are usually found on the south-facing edges of clearings or along the south-facing edges of rides and footpaths. They are located there to catch as much sun as it goes around the southern sky, because the nests are solar radiators keeping the colonies warm. The nests are shaped, sometimes more than a metre across, like misshapen domes made from twigs, pine needles, leaf fragments and leaf and grass stalks. They are absolutely teeming with life and it has been estimated that one nest can contain as many as 300,000 ants. The common cow-wheat, which flowers over an extended period, is an ancient woodland indicator and is uncommon in Sheffield's

Common cow-wheat.

ancient woods. Like most wildlife in Britain, common cow-wheat has its own folklore. It used to be believed that eating the seeds of this plant would ensure that pregnant women would give birth to boys!

At the northern end of the wood is a sunken lane that climbs up the slope to the top of the wood, called Burying Lane. The lane was called Burying Lane because it was a route in which coffins were brought from outlying parts of Ecclesfield parish to St Mary's Parish Church in Ecclesfield village. This part of the wood also has some 'medusoid' trees. Medusoid growth is a particularly noticeable form of neglected coppice, although it may also occur in exposed locations in upland areas as a low-growing single-stemmed tree. This type of worked tree is characterized by its sprawling and contorted growth forms with its branches growing in a 'corkscrew' fashion. It is so named after Medusa, the monster of Greek mythology who instead of hair had a nest of writhing snakes.

Before leaving Grenoside a diversion into another of its ancient woods confronts the visitor with a bit of a surprise. The wood is Prior Royd and the surprise is an enormous crater – and it is not hard to find. It is said to be a bomb crater created by a bomb dropped from a German aircraft in the Second World War.

A watercolour of Burying Lane in Greno Wood by Allan Womersley.

H

Hill Fort at Wincobank

Wincobank Hill dominates the Lower Don valley. It rises at its highest point to only just over 500 ft (153 m) but as the land slopes away very steeply in all directions its presence is felt for some miles around – especially to the south-east in the Don and Rother valleys where the land is flat or gently undulating.

At the summit of the hill is the hill fort. It consists of an oval defensive enclosure of just over 2.5 acres (one hectare) surrounded by a single rampart with an external ditch. The material from the excavated ditch has been thrown up into an outer bank. Today the grass-covered rampart, which at one point rises around 9 feet (2.8 metres) above the bottom of the ditch, is more or less complete except for three breaks, through two of which – in the south-west and north-east – passes a long-established track, called Wincobank Wood Lane. The ditch and outer bank are absent along most of the western side of the fort and along the northern half of the eastern side.

A view of Wincobank Hill.

Possible arrangement of the rampart wall at Wincobank Hill Iron Age camp.

Excavations by Sheffield City Museums in 1899 and 1979 have shown that the rampart was originally built as a very substantial stone wall. The interior of the wall was composed of earth and sandstone rubble bonded together by timbers. The inner side of the wall was faced by small unmortared dressed stones, and the outer side by large, unmortared dressed stones. It is not clear how high the original rampart was, but it would almost certainly have been topped by a timber palisade. No excavations have been made inside the fort and so whether there are any signs of occupation in the form of postholes for buildings or storage or other pits is unknown. When the excavations were made in the rampart, charred timbers were recovered, and in the rubble core there were signs of vitrification, i.e., the filling had been fused into a glass-like substance by intense heat. The charring suggests that the rampart was destroyed by fire.

Using a scientific technique called radiocarbon dating (C14) it is possible to put an approximate date on some archaeological objects. Charcoal from burnt timber taken from the rampart in 1979 gives an approximate date of 500 BC. This suggests that the main rampart was built in the middle of the Iron Age. It was probably built as a result of conflict between neighbouring tribes wishing to control the Don valley. There is also evidence that the hilltop had been frequented at a much earlier date than the Iron Age. Mesolithic (Middle Stone Age, c. 8,000–3,000 BC) flint tools have been found on the hilltop. These would have been made by a moving band of hunter-gatherers who made virtually no impact on the environment that they inhabited.

Wincobank Hill is not only an important historic site; it is also a wonderful vantage point. To the south-west and west there are views over the northern suburbs of Sheffield and to the north-west to the woods beyond Grenoside. To the north across Blackburn Brook is the wooded Grange Park and beyond that Keppel's Column and the spire of Wentworth church. Turning to the north-east, Canklow Wood in Rotherham can be clearly seen. Looking to the south-east there are clear views up the Lower Don valley from Blackburn Meadows and the M1 motorway to Hyde Park and Park Hill flats and the city centre. Directly in front is the Lower Don valley, once the home of Sheffield's heavy steel industry. In the last twenty years the valley has been transformed. Dominating the eastern end of the valley, beside the M1 motorway on the site of Hadfield's East Hecla steelworks is the Meadowhall Shopping Centre, with its 270 stores and free parking for 12,000 cars.

I

Interesting Inn Names

Before shop and public house names came into being, all that existed were shop and pub pictorial signs – proclaiming to all those customers who could not read what their trade was. And these signs are as old as civilisation itself – no fewer than 900 were found in the ruins of Herculaneum, which was destroyed by the eruption of Vesuvius in AD 79. And in some countries shop signs are common to this day.

But let's get back to the main subject – pub names. There are many different categories of pub name. First there are the names that simply tell you that the place sells wine and/or ale. An early inn sign was a bush of vine leaves or a bunch of grapes and this has translated into the modern pub names such as the Grapes Inn in Trippet Lane and in Burngreave. Another common sign was a beer barrel and there is still a Barrel Inn at Lane End, Chapeltown, and another on London Road. The arms of the Vitners Company (the London guild of wine merchants) included three barrels or tuns, and this gave rise to the popular pub name of The Three Tuns.

Then there are the pub names telling us that the pub originally belonged (and may still belong) to the lord of the manor or was leased from him or built on his land. These usually have the name 'So and So's Arms' and the sign is the coat of arms of the lord of the manor. For example, in Sheffield there were once more than a dozen public houses called the Norfolk Arms because the Duke of Norfolk was the major landowner, Arundel and Surrey were named after the Duke's minor titles, the Wharncliffe Arms in Burncross was on land owned by the earls of Wharncliffe of Wortley Hall, the Devonshire Arms on land owned by the Duke of Devonshire of Chatsworth and the Bagshawe Arms on land owned by the Bagshawe family of Norton.

There are also pub names that simply reflect where they are, like The Beeley Wood, the Bridge Inn (at least eight locally) and the Stocks on Stocks Hill in Ecclesfield. There are also religious names, which may seem curious, but in medieval times there was often a close relationship between the church and the local inn with the churchwarden often acting as brewer. There is the The Abbey, The Angel (there are at least seven in the local region) and the Cross Keys (which was the sign of St Peter) at Handsworth.

Royal names are widespread showing patriotism and royal allegiance and it is surprising how many go back into medieval times. These include the White Hart

Inn sign at the Wharncliffe Arms, Burncross.

(heraldic badge of Richard II who made pub signs compulsory in 1393), The Albert Inn (Darnall), the Old Queen's Head (alluding to Mary, Queen of Scots who was held prisoner in Sheffield by the Earl of Shrewsbury for fourteen years), Prince of Wales, Royal George, Red Lion (heraldic badge of John of Gaunt), and Fleur de Lys (associated with Edward II who was king of England and France). Famous people also have pubs named after them of course, for example, The Wellington at Shalesmoor, Shakespeare (at Hillsborough and now called 'The Shakey'), Admiral Rodney at Loxley and Robin Hood at Millhouses.

There is a very large number of pubs named after animals and birds – traditional ones are often being associated with sports (cruel and field sports) such as the Black Bear, the Cock Inn, Dog & Partridge, Hare & Hounds, The Pheasant, The Stag and The Greyhound. Then there are the comical ones like The Fat Cat, Ferret and Trouserleg, and Frog and Parrot. Naturally there are also many inn names linked to transport and travel and these are well represented in Sheffield: the Packhorse Inn, The Wagon & Horses, The Travellers Rest, The Viaduct and the Railway Hotel. It is surprising how few inn names reflect local industry. Ones still surviving include the Cross Scythes, the Hammer and Pincers, The Anvil, The Old Grindstone and the Miners' Arms.

The most interesting names are, of course, the ones with a fascinating personal story attached to them. Take for example the Shepley Spitfire at Totley. This relatively

Shepley Spitfire public house with an aircraft just visible on the wind vane.

new public house (built in 1979) on Mickley Lane has a name that takes us back to the Second World War and a local hero. It is named in memory of Douglas Shepley, third son of Jack and Emily Shepley of Woodthorpe Hall, a few hundred metres to the south in Holmesfield parish in Derbyshire. Douglas was a Spitfire pilot who was shot down over the Channel in August 1940 and his body was never recovered. With the unstinting help of the local community, the Shepley family raised thousands of pounds in his memory to fund the building of a new spitfire. This too was shot down in 1942.

The public house called The Noose & Gibbet on Broughton Lane that runs beside Sheffield Arena in the Lower Don valley not far from Meadowhall Shopping Centre has an altogether different origin. It is named after Spence Broughton, who robbed the Rotherham mail coach on Attercliffe Common in 1791. He was arrested and hanged at York in 1792 and his body gibbeted, 'suspended between heaven and earth' on the common. It is said that 40,000 people turned up the next day to see the gibbeted body. The body hung there for thirty-six years. The gibbet chains still survive. Poems and ballads were written about him. At The Noose & Gibbet public house an effigy of the gibbeted body hangs outside!

Above: The Noose & Gibbet Inn.

Left: A replica of the figure of Spence Broughton hanging on a gibbet.

J

Jawbone Hill

The top of Jawbone Hill lying at 816 feet above the Don valley between Grenoside and Oughtibridge affords a wonderful vantage point. To the south and south-west there are clear views over Sheffield including such easily identified landmarks as Hillsborough Stadium, the University Arts Tower, the whole of the city centre with the town hall and the two cathedrals, and beyond to the Gleadless valley, Norton Water Tower and Herdings flats. Turning to the west and north-west is the rolling hill country between Worrall and Bolsterstone, an area of outstanding beauty in which the small stone-walled fields, winding lanes, hamlets and isolated farms and valley woodlands form a perfect complement to the natural landscape. Beyond that rises the exposed and relatively treeless plateau between Ewden Beck and the Little Don.

So how did Jawbone Hill, or as it is also known, Whalejaw Hill, get its name? Some accounts suggest that actual whales' jawbones once stood at the top of the hill but there is no firm evidence for this assertion. Just as likely is that it got its name because

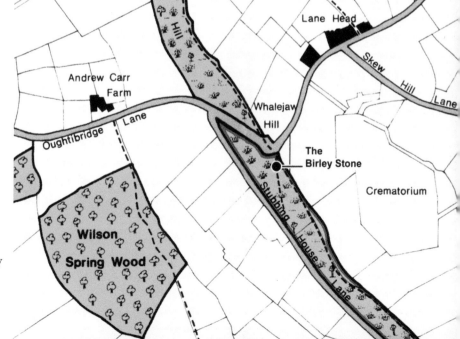

Jawbone Hill and the Birley Stone.

the bend in the lane forms the perfectly symmetrical shape that would have been formed by erecting whale jawbones as an arch.

At the top of Jawbone Hill there is also an important medieval boundary stone. It was first recorded – as *Burleistan* – in a boundary agreement in 1161 between Richard de Lovetot, lord of the manor of Hallamshire, and the monks of the Abbey of St Wandrille in Normandy. This abbey had been granted land in the ancient parish of Ecclesfield and monks from the abbey had founded Ecclesfield Priory by 1273. In the boundary agreement, the monks were to have the freedom to pasture their flocks of sheep and cattle from January to August in a great wood that covered the valley side as far as the *Doun* (the River Don) from *Wereldsend* (Wardsend) to *Uhtinabrigg* (Oughtibridge). The monks were also permitted to pasture their swine (this practice was called pannage) on the fallen acorns in the same wood in the autumn. The remnants of this great wood remain as Wilson Spring Wood and Beeley Wood.

The base of the stone may be the original medieval one, but the shaft is later. Indeed, the original stone may not have been a straight stone shaft, but a stone cross to mark the way from Ecclesfield to Bradfield via Oughtibridge and Worrall. In this case it probably already stood in its present position when the 1161 boundary agreement was drawn up. The stone later became a boundary marker between the Grenofirth and Southey quarters of Ecclesfield parish.

Birley Stone and the surrounding area is part of the Pennine 'stone country'. Solid rock can be seen outcropping at the side of the road opposite the Birley Stone.

The Birley Stone (right) and the Festival Stone (left).

On a short walk to the south along the footpath towards Back Edge outcrops of rock abound and soon the path is diverted by mounds of soil and rock waste from disused quarries. And everywhere are dry stone walls dividing one field from another. This is because the long slope from Birley Edge down to the River Don is underlain by thin seams of coal inter-bedded with shales and massive beds of coal measure sandstones – Greenmor Rock, Grenoside Sandstone and Penistone Flags.

The Second World War also made its temporary mark on the landscape at the top of Jawbone Hill. The area to the east of the Birley Stone, now occupied largely by the crematorium, was an ammunition depot with the ammunition hidden underground in grass-covered bunkers. Here were stored the bombs used in raids on Hitler's Germany and taken on a regular basis by convoys of lorries to the airfields in Lincolnshire. All that is left to remind us of this important part of the war effort are a number of marker stones showing the boundary of the site. There is, immediately behind the Birley Stone, on the edge of the copse, a boundary stone with the initials W D (War Department) on the far side.

Beside the Birley Stone stands the Festival Stone, so called because it was erected by Wortley Rural District Council (Grenoside until 1974 was not part of the City of Sheffield) to celebrate the Festival of Britain in 1951. This is topped by what has variously been called a 'topograph', or a 'toposcope', which is a display showing the direction and distance from the stone of natural and built landmarks.

Rock outcrop with contorted oak tree on Birley Edge.

Kelham Island Industrial Museum

The name Kelham Island refers to the half a mile-long man-made island that resulted from the construction of a mill-race (known locally as a goit) in the twelfth century, which diverted water from the River Don to the waterwheel of the manorial corn mill and then back into the river. 'Kelham' is named after Kelham Horner, the town armourer, who had a grinding workshop on the island in the seventeenth century.

Opened in 1982, the museum, which tells the story of Sheffield's industrial development, occupies the old electricity generating station built in 1899 for the electric tramway system. On approaching the museum the visitor is greeted by the sight of a Bessemer converter. The Bessemer converter made its first appearance on Carlisle Street at Bessemer's Steel Works in 1858. This was a radical step by its inventor, Henry Bessemer, following the sceptical reception of the new invention by the rather conservative Sheffield steel producers. The scepticism arose from doubts about the quality of the large amounts of steel that were produced in a short space of time. Using traditional methods of converting pig iron into blister steel and then into crucible steel took fourteen or fifteen days to produce a 40–50-pound ingot of cast steel, whereas the Bessemer process could produce 6 tons of cast steel in around thirty minutes. Bessemer, the outsider, saw his new works initially as a place of demonstration for potential licensees. Two of Sheffield's major firms, John Brown's and Charles Cammell's, became the earliest converts and produced their first Bessemer steel rails in 1861, followed by Samuel Fox in 1863.

Among the many highlights of the museum, four in particular must be specifically mentioned. These are the River Don Engine, the Hawley Collection, the Simplex car and the 'little mester' workshops. The River Don Engine is a steam engine of 12,000 horsepower that dates from 1905. It originally powered an armour plate rolling mill at Cammell's Grimesthorpe Works. In its latter working years at the British Steel Corporation's River Don Works it rolled steel for nuclear reactors. There are regular demonstrations of the massive engine in operation. The Hawley Collection is an internationally important collection of artefacts, archive material, tapes, films and photographs recording the history of toolmaking, cutlery manufacture and silversmithing in Sheffield. Ken Hawley (1927–2014) collected the material

Above: Bessemer converter at Kelham Island Industrial Museum. (Courtesy of Sheffield Industrial Museums Trust)

Right: The River Don Engine at Kelham Island Industrial Museum. (Courtesy of Sheffield Industrial Museums Trust)

Exhibit showing forging at Kelham Island Industrial Museum. (Courtesy of Sheffield Industrial Museums Trust)

over a fifty-year period. It is housed in the Hawley Gallery that opened in 2010. For a short period between 1908 and 1925 Sheffield had its own car industry. Simplex cars owned by Earl Fitzwilliam of Wentworth Woodhouse produced luxury cars and motorcycles at their car works in Tinsley, and two of the few surviving examples of a Simplex car, one dating from 1908 and the other from 1920, may be examined in the museum at close quarters. Finally there are the little mesters' workshops. In one of these works is Stan Shaw, now in his early nineties, who has a full order book for his beautifully crafted hand-made knives, and in another, Peter Goss, who specialises in the production of forged forceps, hip replacements and bone levers.

L

Lady's Bridge and Loxley Common

The early town of Sheffield extended northwards across the River Don via Sembly Green and along the Wicker via the stone-built **Lady's Bridge**, constructed in 1486 to replace an earlier timber structure. This late medieval bridge, which is hidden below the modern bridge, stood the test of time and attests to the excellent craftsmanship of its builder, master mason William Hyll, and to the critical eye of local citizens. Hyll's instructions in his agreement for building the structure was that he should 'make a suffycient brigge over the watyr of Dune neghe the castell of Sheffield, wele and suffyciently after the sight of workmen of the same crafte and gode men of the parysh'. Lady's Bridge is named after the Chapel of Our Blessed Lady of the Bridge, which once stood to the south of the river under the castle walls.

An early engraving of Lady's Bridge built in 1486, now hidden below the modern bridge.

Lady's Bridge today.

Loxley Common, together with the conterminous Wadsley Common, is a most interesting fragment of common land from historical, archaeological and ecological points of view. The area in question covers the valley side to the north of the River Loxley with Loxley Edge, a sandstone escarpment outcropping in the eastern half of the site and with a boulder-strewn slope below it. Loxley Common is variously referred to in historical documents as Loxley Common, Loxley Chase and Loxley Firth. Loxley Common was mentioned in a late thirteenth-century document in which Thomas de Furnival, the lord of Hallamshire, granted common rights to the inhabitants of the area. In 1332 on the death of Thomas de Furnival it was recorded that the pannage of the woods (*pannagium boscorum*), i.e. the pasturing of pigs on acorns, at 'Rivelyngden and Lokesley' was worth forty shillings. Just over 300 years later in 1637 it was recorded in John Harrison's survey of the manor of Sheffield as 'A Common Called Loxley wood & ffirth' and covered 1,517 acres (614 ha). In 1650 the common was referred to as 'one Great wood called Loxley the herbage common and consisteth of great Oake timber'. Two ancient oak pollards still survive on the site.

It was on Loxley Common that the lord of the manor had his rabbit warrens where he kept his rabbits, which he would have prized for their meat and their fur. There is an entry in the estate accounts in 1724 that states in May of that year Edward Wilson

Above: Loxley Common.

Right: Ancient oak pollard on Loxley Common.

was paid five shillings for 'mending rabit burrs on Loxley and looking after the Rabits there'. If you visit Loxley Common look for the wide double walls with stone on the outside and infilled with rubble and soil. These may be the boundaries of the Loxley Common rabbit warren.

Then there's the Robin Hood connection. Everyone will know that Robin Hood was sometimes referred to as Robin of Loxley or Locksley. Was he a real person? According to some researchers there must have been a real person called Robin or Robert Hood no later than the first half of the thirteenth century but it seems then to have become a name used for an outlaw. It is as if every magician became known as Paul Daniels and every abrupt TV interviewer became known as Jeremy Paxman. The connection with Loxley, however, goes further than the name. In the survey of the manor of Sheffield carried out in 1637 already referred to above, which was described by its author as 'Exact and Perfect', was recorded 'ye foundacion of a house or Cottage where Robin Hood was borne'!

Most of Loxley Common was in the ownership of the Payne family from 1800. In 1913, three surviving family sisters presented 75½ acres (30.5 ha) of the common to the City of Sheffield provided it retained its semi-rural character and was used as a public open space. In the 1970s it was designated a Site of Scientific Interest and it became a Local Nature Reserve in 1999, because of its status as lowland heath, an increasingly rare and threatened habitat. A Friends group, the Wadsley and Loxley Commoners, undertake workdays throughout the year, removing invading birch and bracken.

Manor Lodge, Meersbrook and the Millennium Galleries and Winter Garden

The **Manor Lodge** is located on a high point near the centre of the former Sheffield deer park. The deer park was one of the biggest in the country, extending to 2,460 acres and 8 miles (13 kilometres) in circumference. As late as 1637 there were 1,000 fallow deer in the park. Manor Lodge was originally a lodge for the park keeper that was converted into a comfortable country residence by George, the 4th Earl of Shrewsbury (1468–1538).

The lodge is mostly in ruins now. As you enter the site today from the visitor centre you walk across what would have been an entrance area that once contained stables and a guardroom into the inner court. Running along the southern edge of this former courtyard are the ruins of what would have been kitchens and storage cellars. On your right running northwards are the remains of the wall of the long gallery which had apartments in towers at the northern and southern ends. The site of the northern tower has become known as the Wolsey Tower because this was where Cardinal Wolsey stayed for eighteen days in 1529 on his journey from York to London. He had fallen out of favour with King Henry VIII because he had failed to get permission from the Pope for Henry to divorce Catherine of Aragon. He was charged with treason but died shortly after leaving Sheffield before he could be brought to trial.

Beyond the inner court was the outer court in which the three-storeyed Turret House built in the mid-1570s still survives largely intact. On an upper floor of the Turret House is a room with an original Elizabethan fireplace and decorated plaster ceiling. The Manor Lodge is most famous because Mary, Queen of Scots spent much time here during her long imprisonment between 1570 and 1584 under George, 6th Earl of Shrewsbury. Some early writers believed that the Turret House was Mary's prison at the Manor Lodge. It is more likely to have been a banqueting house and a standing or 'prospect house'. A standing was a tower-like structure from which the surrounding landscape could be viewed. Significantly there is a staircase from the second floor up to the roof. Joseph Hunter writing in 1813 was of no doubt that it was a standing with glorious views of the surrounding countryside: 'The fir-crowned heights of Norton,

Above left: The Turret House, Sheffield Manor. (Courtesy of Green Estate)

Above right: Interior of the turret house showing the fine plaster ceiling. (Courtesy of Green Estate)

the sweet vale of Beauchief, the purple moors of Totley, the barren hills of the Peak, the thick woods of Wharncliffe and Wentworth, the widening vale of the Don... are all comprehended within the view from this elevation.'

One linear historic feature that once terminated at the back of the Turret House was an avenue of walnut trees that stretched as far as the gate that led to the castle at the north-eastern end of the park. The trees were cut down and sold to a Sheffield joiner in 1715. Writing in 1915 Thomas Winder stated that the blackened trunks of three ancient walnut trees still stood behind the Turret House.

Meersbrook contains two very interesting places of historical interest. The timber-framed **Bishops' House** in Norton Lees on the edge of Meersbrook Park is now a museum. This is an L-shaped yeoman's house built by the Blythe family. The western wing (the original house) was long believed to have been constructed between 1500 and 1550, but a recent dendrochronological analysis suggests a date of 1554. An eastern extension was built around 1580 at right angles to the original house. The west wing had a parlour and buttery on the ground floor and two chambers above on the first floor. The east wing contained the hall and the lesser parlour on the ground floor and two chambers on the first floor. The house has a king post roof. The timber framing at ground-floor level has been largely replaced by stone and a northern extension to the west wing was built in stone in the mid-seventeenth century.

A variety of patterns of timber work was employed on the outside of the walls. Herringbone patterns were used on both wings. What is very noticeable is that timbers on the outside of the building (the studs) are closely spaced, with the spaces not much wider than the studs themselves. This close studding is a typical characteristic of timber-framed buildings in the north of England. The spaces between the studs at Bishops' House were filled with split oak laths and then covered with plaster. Inside the house there are several interesting features including carpenters' marks, adze marks on the shaped timber beside the stairhead and thick oak planks to make the floorboards in the east wing of seventeenth-century date.

To the south of Bishops' House lies the 45-acre **Meersbrook Park** from which there are wonderful panoramic views of the city. The park surrounds Meersbrook Hall, once the home of a succession of prosperous merchants. The park was opened as a municipal park in 1885 and between 1890 and 1953 the hall housed the Ruskin Museum. After being used for a period by Sheffield City Council's Parks and Countryside Service, the Friends of Meersbrook Hall and Heeley Development Trust are now working together to keep it in public ownership in ways that benefit the local community. The park contains its old **walled kitchen garden** run by Meersbrook Park Users Trust and Heeley City Farm since 1999. For many years used as a car park and rubbish dump, the garden has been transformed and now contains a lawn, a large greenhouse and even a Japanese garden. Volunteers maintain the garden and courses and special events take place on a regular basis.

The **Millennium Galleries**, completed in 2001 as part of the 'Heart of the City' project, have three complementary roles. First and foremost, they extend the city's museum space

Bishops' House.

Above: Furnished bedroom, Bishops' House.

Below: The Japanese garden in Meersbrook Park walled garden.

The 'bug hotel' in Meersbrook Park walled garden.

by nearly 2,000 square metres; together with the adjoining Winter Garden, they form an interesting covered section on the route from the railway station and Sheffield Hallam University to the urban centre; and the café is a pleasant place to have a refreshing drink or a light snack. The Millennium Galleries face onto Arundel Gate with the café on the ground floor. The galleries occupy the upper floor and are reached from Arundel Gate by escalator. Along with temporary exhibitions there is a permanent space for Sheffield's metalwork and silverware collection and the Ruskin Collection. The latter is the property of the Guild of St George, an organisation set up by John Ruskin 'to broaden the minds of working people', which established its first museum in Sheffield in 1875.

The adjoining **Winter Garden** was and is the crowning glory of the £120m 'Heart of the City' project. It is a place to meet or relax for workers and shoppers alike in a very unusual environment combining stunning architecture with a unique collection of plants. The new structure was opened in December 2002 with a children's candlelight procession and fireworks and within a year had attracted more than one million visitors. It is 230 ft (70 m) long and 72 ft (22 m) wide and its arched structure is formed by pairs of parabolic wooden arches that reach up to 72 ft (22 m). There are ten pairs of arches, made of larch, which require no preservative coatings and which will mature to a silvery grey colour. It is a temperate glasshouse with the temperature kept constant, frost kept at bay and humidity closely controlled. This is achieved in a number of ways. The building is glazed with more than 1,400 glass panels, of which 128 open and close automatically. Fans move concentrations of hot air in summer which is then released through the vents. Underfloor heating protects the plants from frost and small water features control levels of humidity. The Winter Garden houses 2,500 plants of over 150 species mainly from the Southern Hemisphere including palms from Madagascar, grass trees from Australia and pines from Norfolk Island. Drought-resistant plants are concentrated at the southern end of the glasshouse, which gets most sun, and shade lovers at the northern end. The plants are in beds that contain 400 tons of soil. Most of the plants bloom in winter – hence the name Winter Garden.

Above: The Winter Garden.

Below: Exterior view of the Winter Garden.

National Emergency Services Museum and Norton

The **National Emergency Services Museum** is housed in an old police, fire and ambulance station on the corner of West Bar and Tenter Street just outside the city centre. The museum opened in 1984 as the Sheffield Fire and Police Museum and

Exterior view of the National Emergency Services Museum showing the Fire Brigade observation tower.

became the National Emergency Services Museum in 2014. Before entering the museum there is a rare structure to be seen: one of only two surviving Fire Brigade observation towers at the Tenter Street end of the building.

Inside the museum the visitor can inspect at close quarters more than forty old vehicles ranging from horse-drawn fire engines to police cars and ambulances. It is a 'hands-on' museum and children can climb in and out of vehicles and try on uniforms. And there is even a lifeboat, *The City of Sheffield*, that was built in the 1980s using £420,000 raised in Sheffield. The boat has seen service at Whitby, Ramsgate, Hartlepool, Sennen Cove and Poole. During its service at Poole between 2001 and 2015 it was launched on more than 500 occasions and used to rescue 656 people.

If you are not into vehicles, you can enter and feel what it must have been like to be locked up in a small police cell in the past. And, with the dramatic use of lights, sound and smoke you can step into the reality of a road traffic incident, a street fire or a house fire.

The village, now the outer suburb, of **Norton** was originally not in South Yorkshire but in the ancient county of Derbyshire. Its village origins are most obvious when you stand in the well-treed churchyard looking towards the medieval church. You

An early fire engine in the National Emergency Services Museum. (Courtesy of the NES Museum)

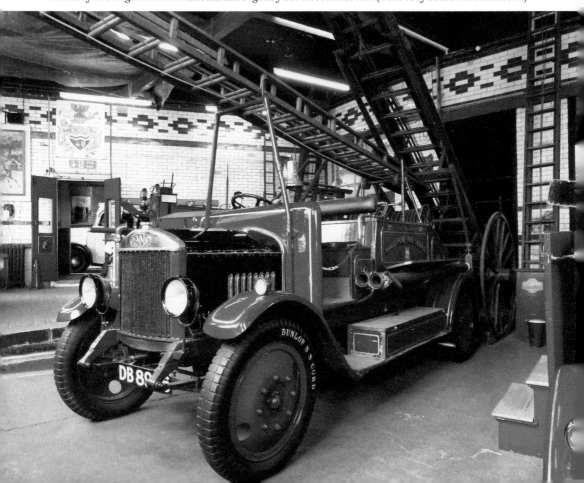

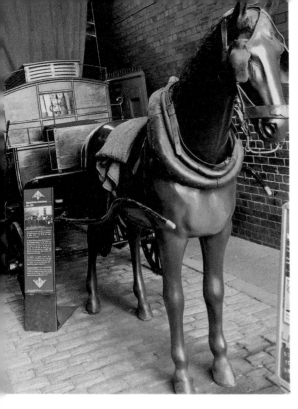

The first Barnsley horse-drawn ambulance (1885) currently on display in the National Emergency Services Museum as part of the 'Blood, Bandages and Blue Lights' exhibition. (Courtesy of the NES Museum)

can well imagine that you are still standing in the centre of a rural village. Outside the churchyard there are other signs of Norton's rural and semi-rural origins. Oakes Park, set in its extensive grounds and now a Christian activity centre for young people, dates from 1688 and was the ancestral home of the Bagshawe family for 288 years. Another reminder of the Bagshawe family is the Bagshawe Arms, which has operated as a public house since 1844. Another country house, Norton Hall, now converted into high-quality apartments, was built c. 1815 by the banker Samuel Shore, and in the second half of the nineteenth century it became the home of the Sheffield industrialist Charles Cammell and then Bernard Alexander Firth, the son of another famous Sheffield industrialist, Mark Firth. Norton Hall's extensive parkland with its woods and lakes was bought by Alderman J. G. Graves, the city's best-known public benefactor, and in 1925 he offered it to the City Council as a public park, Graves Park, which now covers more than 220 acres. In 1976 22 acres of land adjacent to the park was acquired and the Rare Breeds Centre was established. This was replaced by the Graves Animal Farm in 1995.

Then there is the parish church itself, St James', whose existence was first recorded in 1183. Substantial rebuilding of the earliest church took place between the twelfth and fifteenth centuries when aisles and a porch were added. Extensive restoration took place in 1882. The church porch is full of interest. The arch above the door has some of the original Norman zigzag moulding; there are six corbel stones with crudely carved faces and there are several seventeenth-century tombstones. Inside a close examination of the font is called for. On its eastern face is a carving of a salamander, representing the devil angered by the Christian baptisms taking place. In the Blythe Chapel, built around 1524, is a carved alabaster monument to William and Saffrey

56

Above: St James' Church, Norton.

Below: The Blythe Chapel in St James' Church, Norton.

Blythe. The chapel was built by their son, Geoffrey Blythe, Bishop of Lichfield. The Blythe family owned and farmed land in Norton Lees for more than three centuries from around 1377 and are the family associated with Bishops' House (see above).

The most famous son of Norton, Sir Francis Chantrey (1781–1841), is also commemorated on a plaque in the chancel and a sculpture in the nave. Chantrey was born in Jordanthorpe in the parish, the son of a carpenter and small farmer. He was educated, irregularly, in the village school and was a milk-boy going regularly into Sheffield with his donkey to deliver milk, butter and eggs before returning with his mother's shopping. He was apprenticed to a grocer in Sheffield but was soon attracted by the nearby shop window of a carver and gilder and Chantrey persuaded his parents to let him be apprenticed to the carver instead of the grocer. By 1802 he was released from his apprenticeship and set up as a portrait painter. He soon gave this up and concentrated on sculpture. He became 'the chosen sculptor of monarchs and statesmen' as local writer Harold Armitage put it. Among his subjects were George IV, Sir Walter Scott, the Duke of Wellington and William Pitt. His most celebrated work is *The Sleeping Children* in Lichfield Cathedral. He was knighted by William IV in 1835. He insisted in being buried in Norton churchyard, having personally chosen his burial plot there. In 1854 the 28-foot-high 'Chantrey obelisk', simply inscribed 'Chantrey', was erected on what was left of Norton village green.

Statue of Sir Francis Chantrey in St James' Church, Norton.

O

Oaks Fold Cruck Barn and the Old Queen's Head

In Concord Park in Shiregreen stands **Oaks Fold cruck barn.** This is now a ranger base. If the rangers are there they will be happy to show you around the interior. Cruck buildings were common in the upland areas of Britain and parts of the Midlands but

The exterior of Oaks Fold Barn with the wooden carving of a wolf. (The meaning of Woolley in the nearby Woolley Wood means a woodland clearing frequented by wolves.)

Interior of Oaks Fold Barn.

are virtually unknown in eastern and south-eastern England. In a cruck building the weight was carried on pairs of timbers called cruck blades, which rise from or near the ground and meet at the apex of the roof. The blades are usually curved, having been selected from naturally bent trees. Often a bent tree was split or sawn lengthways to make two matching blades. The structure was strengthened by tie beams connecting each pair of cruck blades. The roof of the building was stabilised by struts called windbraces. The walls consisted of vertical studs rising from the sill beam to the wall plates with the gaps filled with a variety of materials as already noted or covered with horizontal oak boarding. Oaks Fold cruck barn was described in Harrison's survey of the manor of Sheffield in 1637 as 'a Barne of 5 bayes'. A bay was the space between each pair (in this case six) of cruck blades. The cruck blades are on full view and at the west end of the barn the lath and plaster wall filling can be seen.

In the north-western corner of Sheffield's enormous deer park, beside the fish ponds which eventually formed the water power for the lord of the manor's second corn mill, stood the Hall in the Ponds, which survives in part today as the **Old Queen's Head** public house.

Dendrochronological (tree-ring) analysis shows that this timber-framed building was built of timber felled between 1503–10. The building is jettied on the south, west and east sides, has close-studded walls, a king post roof and carved heads on the exterior of the ground-floor posts. The two-storeyed building originally had a single two-bayed room on each floor, with the first-floor room open to the roof.

In an inventory of its contents compiled in 1582 the building was said to contain 'peces of paynted hangings' and window and chimney pieces of canvas, a trestle table, two 'buffet formes', a 'buffet stoule', a still, a flagon, pewter dishes and a spit, all suggesting it was used for the preparation of meals and dining in a very comfortable setting. It may originally have been a banqueting house for the lord of the manor and his guests at the end of a day's hunting, fishing and fowling in the park. Significantly, in a letter from an estate official in Sheffield to the 7th Earl of Shrewsbury and his Countess in 1599 (who were in London) an account is given of stocking with fish 'the Pond mill dam' for the Earl's use.

Above: The Old Queen's Head public house.

Right: Carved head on the exterior of the
Old Queen's Head.

Porter Valley

A walk along the middle and upper reaches of the Porter Valley can be both relaxing and informative. The public footpath follows the river all the way from Hunter's Bar to Fulwood Head and is relatively flat except for the far western section through Porter Clough. At various points roads have to be crossed. In this part of its course the Porter flows through a public park, beside ancient woodlands and through an impressive stand of conifers and broadleaves planted on steep slopes in the narrowest part of the valley. In part of the upper section of its course the river flows through the picturesque Mayfield Valley, a landscape of farms. At the western end of its route at Fulwood Head, and at other points between Porter Clough and Carr Bridge, there are magnificent views over Sheffield. The valley has a rich birdlife with eighty species recorded including dippers, herons and grey wagtails and evening strollers are likely to see Daubenton bats feeding over the ponds and Noctule bats circling at treetop level.

Between Hunter's Bar and Oakbrook Road the river flows through Endcliffe Park. The bulk of the area that is now the park was acquired by the Corporation in 1885 and designed by William Goldring, a nationally acclaimed park designer, who kept, as instructed, as much of the semi-natural landscape as possible. It incorporates Endcliffe Wood, the fragment of an ancient woodland. The park also contains two former water-powered industrial sites with the ponds (locally called dams) still intact. Holme Wheel Dam, the first to be encountered on a walk from Hunter's Bar, was attached to a mill that operated until 1900 but by 1903 was in use as a boating lake. The second dam, Nether Spur-Gear Wheel Dam, provided the water for a grinding mill that had seventeen grinding troughs in 1830. It has now been converted into a refuge for wildfowl. Occupying the southern hillside across Rustlings Road between Holme Wheel Dam and Shepherd Wheel is another park, Bingham Park, which incorporates another ancient wood, Trippett Wood. The bulk of Bingham Park was a gift in 1911 by Sir John Bingham, senior partner of Walker & Hall, one of Sheffield's largest cutlery and silversmithing firms.

Having crossed Oakbrook Road, the visitor to the Porter Valley can stroll beside Trippett Wood towards Shepherd Wheel, a must for anyone interested in industrial archaeology. The first mention of this industrial site was in 1566 and it worked commercially until 1930. Its name is derived from Edward Shepherd who operated the works during the second half of the eighteenth century. It is now a museum and is open to the public every weekend. The two workshops are preserved, the dam is kept full and the waterwheel is operated regularly.

While watching the waterwheel turn and inspecting the workshops with its grinding hulls it is also necessary to consider the working conditions inside this workplace located in what would have been a semi-rural location. The grinders who worked there would have been exposed to major health hazards. The main cause of death among grinders was grinders' asthma, caused by the inhalation of stone and metal dust. In the 1830s life expectancy among fork grinders who ground on dry grindstones was between twenty-eight and thirty-two.

Beyond Shepherd Wheel the footpath runs beside Whiteley Woods, which contain Wire Mill Dam, where there were once two dams constructed by Thomas Boulsover, the inventor of Old Sheffield Plate. There is a monument to Boulsover by the surviving dam. Half a mile farther up the valley just beyond the western edge of Whiteley Woods is Forge Dam, the former site of a forge also once owned by Thomas Boulsover but better known in the past as a boating lake. Beyond Forge Dam the valley opens up into the Mayfield Valley, a farmed landscape with farms, cottages, shelter belts and walled and hedged fields. Finally, after a steep walk through the Porter Clough Plantation the trail ends at Fulwood Lane on the boundary of the Peak District National Park.

The dam at Shepherd Wheel. (Courtesy of Sheffield Industrial Museums Trust)

Above: The waterwheel at Shepherd Wheel. (Courtesy of Sheffield Industrial Museums Trust)

Below: Forge Dam when it was a boating lake as portrayed on an old postcard.

Quarry Gardens at Whinfell

Whinfell Quarry Gardens lie in south-west Sheffield 4 miles from the city centre on the A625 near the entrance to Whirlow Brook Park. This ornamental garden that covers just over 1 hectare was created in 1898 as part of the extensive grounds of Whinfell House. Samuel Doncaster, a notable local industrialist, had the house built in a half-timbered style and he commissioned the firm of James Backhouse and Son from York Nurseries to supply the plants for the new garden, which consisted of a terraced area with the quarry garden below. The derelict flagstone quarry provided an ideal microclimate for the growing of rare and exotic plants. The quarry has

A general view of Whinfell Quarry Gardens.

Above: Autumn colour in Whinfell Quarry Gardens.

Left: Giant gunnera in Whinfell Quarry Gardens.

steep winding paths and steps, a few rock pools and some rare plants, shrubs and trees including bamboo, giant gunnera, redwoods, weeping beech, cedars, maples, flowering cherries and rhododendrons.

In 1912 Clarence Elliott, a nationally acclaimed horticulturist, plantsman and nurseryman, was commissioned to design a smaller quarry as a limestone rock garden. Here many alpines, shrubs, deciduous trees and conifers were planted. In 1933 Frederick Neill purchased the house from Samuel Doncaster. In the 1960s there were major renovations to the gardens, including extensive replanting. In 1968 the gardens were presented to the city by James Neill Holdings Ltd as a memorial to Sir Frederick Neill. There is a plaque to Sir Frederick to the west of the entrance. In 1971 Whinfell House was destroyed by fire and demolished. Flats now occupy the site of the house. Over the years the gardens suffered through lack of maintenance and deserved greater recognition and funding. In 1999 it was listed as a Grade II Garden of Special Historic Interest by English Heritage. There is now a Friends of Whinfell Quarry Garden group who raise funds and awareness of the gardens and undertake regular working days.

R

Railway Station

Sheffield did not get a direct railway route to London until 1870 when the first station on this site was built. Before that time a railway journey to London involved a trip to Rotherham on the Sheffield and Rotherham Railway, to board a train on the Midland Railway's line from York to London via Derby. The reason for this was that there is a broad ridge between Sheffield and Chesterfield to the south that would have

General view of the entrance to Sheffield railway station.

needed very deep cuttings to be made. Instead George Stephenson took the line to Rotherham through the Rother valley where the gradients were easier. The 1870 line to Chesterfield breaches the high ridge via the Bradway tunnel. The present station, still known to many as the 'Midland Station', is the creation of Charles Trubshaw in 1905, although some of the 1870 station still survives on platform 2. The front elevation of the station is in a classical style with a series of large arched entrances in Derbyshire sandstone. There is some fine decoration in the stonework inside and out. Behind the arched entrances is a large cast-iron roofed porte-cochère. The station underwent refurbishment schemes in 2002, 2008 and again in 2010–11.

It was in 2008 that restoration began on the former refreshment room and dining room on platform 1. These became disused in the 1960s and the refreshment room was converted into a waiting room in the 1970s. By 1976 it became unused and important features such as the mahogany bar and ornate fireplace were removed. The space was vandalised and a leaking roof led to the partial collapse of the ornate plaster ceiling.

The bar in the Sheffield Tap.

The microbrewery at the Sheffield Tap.

Now, with financial assistance from the Railway Heritage Trust, the rooms have been restored back to their Edwardian splendour, and form a fine bar, called the Sheffield Tap, with its own microbrewery. The bar serves beers from all over the world.

Not only has the station itself been refurbished but the townscape outside has undergone a transformation. Gone is the roundabout at the bottom of Howard Street, the office blocks of Sheaf House and Dyson House have been demolished, the line of Sheaf Street has been realigned and immediately in front of the station a new public square, Sheaf Square, has been created. This has water features, trees and public seating. On the edge of the square beside Sheaf Street is a stainless-steel sculpture – the *Cutting Edge*. The sculpture and the station façade are all illuminated at night. Stainless steel was a Sheffield invention in 1913. The discoverer of stainless steel, a chromium steel that almost completely resists corrosion, was locally born (in Ramsden's Yard, off the Wicker) Harry Brearley. He rose from bottle washer to director of Brown-Firth's research laboratories.

Sheffield Cathedral and Sheffield City Hall

The Church of St Peter and St Paul, Sheffield's medieval parish church, became **Sheffield Cathedral** in 1914. The present church initially dates from the early fifteenth century, replacing an earlier church probably of early twelfth-century origin. The crossing tower surmounted by its crocketed spire is an important local landmark. The church was restored between 1878–80 by local architects Flockton & Gibbs with advice from Sir George Gilbert Scott. Ambitious twentieth-century plans in the interwar and post-war periods to make the church more 'cathedral-like' were only partially completed.

The cathedral is a treasure house of monuments and stained glass. The Shrewsbury Chapel contains the tombs of the 4th Earl of Shrewsbury (d. 1538) lying between his two wives and the 6th Earl of Shrewsbury (d. 1590) with his feet resting on a Talbot, a hunting dog bearing the family name. The Chapel of St George has an unusual screen on its eastern side of alternating swords and bayonets, with swords pointing upwards and the bayonets downwards. Among the magnificent stained-glass windows are those by Christopher Webb, most of which relate to Sheffield's history.

In the churchyard is a monument to James Montgomery (1771–1854), newspaper editor and proprietor, campaigner, poet and hymn writer. He campaigned for many years against slavery and the employment of young children as chimney sweeps and wrote the hymn 'Angels from the Realms of Glory'.

Opened in 1932, the **City Hall** was originally designed as early as 1920, by E. Vincent Harris, but construction did not begin until 1929. It has been completely refurbished at a cost of over £12 million. It is built of stone quarried in Darley Dale in the Classical Revival style dominated by the portico with eight Corinthian columns. Originally conceived as a memorial hall to the city's First World War dead, it became Sheffield's main concert hall with a memorial hall at the rear. The main hall accommodates 2,800 people.

There are two important monuments outside the City Hall. In Barkers' Pool stands the war memorial to the 5,000 men who died in the First World War that was unveiled in 1925 arising from a competition announced a year earlier. The competition was

Right: Stained-glass window depicting three former lords of the manor of Sheffield – Waltheof, William de Lovetot and Gerard de Furnival – by Christopher Webb (b. 1866). (By kind permission of the Dean and Chapter of Sheffield Cathedral)

Below: The monument of the 6th Earl of Shrewsbury. (By kind permission of the Dean and Chapter of Sheffield Cathedral)

won by the University of Sheffield's Head of the School of Architecture, C. D. Carus Wilson. It is in the form of a steel pole rising 90 feet (27 metres) from a bronze base. The pole is surrounded by life-size figures of four soldiers with their heads bowed, sculpted by George Alexander. A more recent monument, unveiled in 2016, beside the southern end of the frontage of the City Hall is the statue to the Women of Steel commemorating the vital part that women played in the local steel industry during the two world wars. It was sculpted by Martin Jennings.

Exterior view of Sheffield City Hall.

Above: One of two carved lions, once on the stage and now in the entrance foyer of the City Hall.

Left: Part of the ornate ceiling in the entrance foyer of the City Hall.

T

Tinsley Viaduct and the Town Hall

Many visitors to Sheffield, from the north and the south, know they have arrived in the city when they see (from a train) or cross in a car the **Tinsley Viaduct** carrying the M1 motorway on its upper deck and the A631 on its lower deck. It stretches for 1,003 metres (more than 1 kilometre) between Tinsley in the south to Wincobank in the north crossing the River Don, Sheffield Canal and the Midland Railway line. It was opened in 1968 and cost £6 million. It is of box girder construction. Since its opening the viaduct's support structure has been strengthened on two occasions, completed in 1983 and 2006. Further refurbishment work is currently underway. Until their demolition on 25 August 2008 even more iconic than the viaduct were the two 250-foot-high disused cooling towers that were just 39 feet from the motorway. Built in 1938 as part of Blackburn Meadows power station, the toppling of the two towers, or 'salt and pepper pots' as some locals called them, attracted a crowd estimated at 10,000 at 3 o'clock in the morning. Petitions were signed objecting to the decision to remove the towers and poems were written in memory of the towers and their destruction. One story that was in circulation in the 1990s was that the arts officer in neighbouring Rotherham had applied to the Arts Council for a grant in order to insert giant tulips in each of the towers!

The centre of Sheffield is dominated by the **Town Hall**, built of Derbyshire sandstone, standing at the junction of Surrey Street and Pinstone Street. Designed

Part of Tinsley Viaduct.

Sheffield Town Hall from the Peace Gardens.

by E. W. Mountford, after a competition that prompted 178 entries, it was described by Sir Nicholas Pevsner as 'a large picturesque pile'. The foundation stone was laid in 1891 and it was opened by Queen Victoria on 21 May 1897, who was greeted by Sheffield's first lord mayor, the Duke of Norfolk. It is said that Queen Victoria never left her horse-drawn carriage during the visit. After opening the Town Hall she was driven to Norfolk Park where 50,000 children had been assembled to sing to the queen. According to the local press not many children were lost! The visit ended with a trip to Charles Cammell's Cyclops Steelworks to see armour plate being manufactured for Royal Navy battleships, or as the corporation address stated, 'which guards your Empire upon the sea'. A photograph taken during the Royal visit shows the queen still sitting in her landau watching a sheet of steel emerging from the rollers.

Reflecting Sheffield's industrial history there are two friezes carved in stone around the exterior walls of the Town Hall which depict, among other things, grinders, smiths, smelters and miners. The 200-foot tower is surmounted by an 8-foot-high bronze statue of Vulcan, the Roman god of fire and furnaces, with his right foot on an anvil, a hammer in his right hand and arrows in his left hand. Inside is a life-size statue of Henry Fitzalan-Howard, 15th Duke of Norfolk, Sheffield's first lord mayor, and a bust of Queen Victoria. Beside the Town Hall is a Sheffield curiosity. On the corner of Pinstone Street and Surrey Street stands the last of more than 100 'Dr Who' Tardis police boxes that were once dotted about the city. All it lacks is the blue light on top that flashed when there was an urgent police message. Police boxes like these were introduced from 1928 by celebrated Chief Constable Percy Sillitoe, renowned for bringing the Sheffield 'gang wars' to an end during the interwar years.

U

Underbank Chapel and the Universities

Underbank Chapel stands just beyond the western edge of Stannington at a height of 718 ft (220 m) overlooking the rural Loxley valley. It was built in 1742–43 in local gritstone with a stone-slated roof. On the main front are two tall arched windows originally ranged on either side of the pulpit. On either side of the arched windows are doors with circular windows above. The interior saw many alterations in the nineteenth and twentieth centuries but there is still a gallery at the east end of the chapel. In the past galleries extended round three sides. The caretaker's house sits at right angles to the chapel. Both lie within a graveyard shaded by mature trees. When the modern visitor stands in the grounds of a place of worship in a location like this, the following words from Blake come to mind:

> *And did those feet in ancient time,*
> *Walk upon England's mountains green?*
> *And was the Holy Lamb of God*
> *On England's pleasant pastures seen?*

And across the road is the schoolroom, opened in 1854.

In February 1796 the minister of Underbank Chapel had a surprise visitor. This was Samuel Taylor Coleridge, the poet and author of *The Ancient Mariner* and *Kubla Khan*. He was on a journey across England trying to obtain subscribers to his radical periodical *The Watchman*, which involved him preaching in a Unitarian chapel and giving a public lecture in every town or city that he visited. He came to Sheffield and went to call on the assistant minister of the Upper Chapel in central Sheffield only to find that he had gone to Stannington to visit the minister at Underbank. He later described in great detail his journey back to Sheffield in the dark. He fell into pits and against rocks and got lost. In desperation he knocked on a cottage door only to be faced with what he described as 'a tall old hag' whose ugliness chilled him to the bone. However, she turned out to be an 'angel of light' who arranged for her son to guide him on his way.

The **University of Sheffield** was officially opened by King Edward VII on 12 July 1905. The new university had started life as a university college in 1897, being an

Above: An exterior view of Underbank Chapel.

Left: The interior of Underbank Chapel.

amalgamation of Firth College (which became the School of Arts & Science), the Medical Institution (which became the Medical School) and the Technical School (which became the School of Technology). The commitment to gain full university status had been spurred on when it was mooted that the University College of Leeds should become the University of Yorkshire. The new red-brick university building, Firth Court at Western Bank beside Weston Park, was designed by Mitchell Gibbs in the Tudor style. Dominating the Western Bank campus today is the twenty-one-storey Arts Tower completed in 1965. Modern in every respect when it was built, it

The University of Sheffield Arts Tower from Weston Park.

has a concrete frame and is covered in glass walling. The building presently contains two conventional lifts and a paternoster lift. The latter, open-doored and in continual motion up and down, is said to have deterred some prospective students from taking up the place offered to them at the university.

One of the newer university buildings is the Information Commons, a library and computer centre. The university, which has 26,000 students, has an enviable reputation, receiving in 2001 *The Sunday Times* University of the Year award and being described by *The Times* as one of the powerhouses of British higher education. Among the long list of well-known graduates of the university are pioneer aviator Amy Johnson, the astronaut Helen Sharman, politician David Blunkett and playwright Jack Rosenthal.

Sheffield Hallam University is one of the 'new' universities created in 1992. Its history is long and complicated. Until the 1970s there were a number of colleges in the Sheffield region, each with their own culture and ethos. On the Pond Street site, now the City Campus, was the College of Technology that was created in 1950 and which occupied an expanding site that was built between 1953 and 1968. In 1969 the College of Technology merged with the College of Art, which occupied a site on Psalter Lane 2 miles to the south-west of the city centre, to form Sheffield Polytechnic. Then in 1976 Sheffield Polytechnic merged with the City College of Education and Totley-Thornbridge College, another teacher training institution. Sheffield Polytechnic then became Sheffield City Polytechnic. Finally, Lady Mabel College, a women's PE teacher training college housed in Wentworth Woodhouse in Rotherham, joined Sheffield City Polytechnic in 1979. The varied origins and specialisms of its various component parts has meant that Sheffield Hallam University, from its outset, has been able to offer a very wide range of undergraduate and postgraduate degree courses. It prides itself on its close association with places of work with a high proportion of its students on courses with a work placement.

The City Campus occupies a steeply sloping site in the Sheaf valley between Sheaf Street and Arundel Gate. The cluster of original academic buildings is dominated by the twelve-storey Owen Building, the eight-storey Norfolk Building and the five-storey Surrey Building. At the heart of the campus and linking with adjoining buildings is the five-storeyed, glass-roofed atrium constructed in 1992–93. The ground floor of the atrium forms a gathering place and refreshment area for major events such as public lectures and conferences which use the adjacent Pennine Lecture Theatre. The Adsetts Centre, a library and resources centre occupying a part of the original college site occupied by workshops, was completed in 1997. Since then it has continued to expand, one of its most recent additions in 2016 being the former General Post Office on the edge of Fitzalan Square, which after a £9 million refurbishment now houses the Institute of Arts.

Looking towards Sheffield Hallam University from Sheaf Square.

V

Victoria Quays

Transport developments were crucial in the expansion of the steel industry. In the seventeenth and eighteenth centuries, the products of the Sheffield light steel trades were moved to their markets by packhorse with as many as fifty at a time leaving the town for the ports of Yorkshire and Lancashire. Goods for the London and European market went to the river port of Bawtry where they were transferred to barges and carried down the River Idle to the Trent and the port of Hull. The inconvenience and

Victoria Quays.

The Straddle warehouse at Victoria Quays.

slowness of the overland journey from Sheffield to Bawtry led the Cutlers Company to explore the possibility of making the Don navigable from Doncaster to Sheffield and in 1726 an Act of Parliament was passed and work began. But it proved impracticable at the time to extend the waterway beyond Tinsley and so Tinsley remained the terminus from 1751 until the late date of 1819 when the Sheffield Canal opened, terminating at the canal basin near the junction of the Sheaf and Don. The extension of the canal into Sheffield was greeted with acclaim in the town and a fleet of barges with flags and bands made a triumphal entry into the canal basin. The old canal basin has been renovated and is now the Victoria Quays. It was opened by HRH the Prince of Wales in 1994. It contains offices, a hotel and berths for canal boats. Surviving buildings include the Grade II listed Terminal Warehouse, Straddle Warehouse and a terrace of coal merchants' offices.

W

Weston Park, the Wicker and Woolley Wood

Weston Park was created from the grounds of Weston Hall, an early nineteenth-century house built by Thomas Harrison, a prominent Sheffield saw-maker. The house and grounds were bought by Sheffield Corporation in 1875 and the grounds

The bandstand at Weston Park with Weston Park Museum in the background.

Part of a display in the wildlife gallery of Weston Park Museum. (Courtesy of Museums Sheffield)

were converted into a public park by Robert Marnock. The house became Sheffield's first museum. It was rebuilt in 1935. The museum was closed for renovation in 2003 and reopened in 2006.

The park still retains its rare bandstand, which has been restored to its former glory. Other notable features are an obelisk to the artist and designer Godfrey Sykes, a statue of the 'Corn Law Rhymer' Ebenezer Elliott, and the York and Lancaster War memorial to the almost 9,000 men who lost their lives in the First World War and the 1,200 who died in the Second World War.

The Wicker seems an odd name for a street. It is probably derived from the Old Danish word for a willow tree, exactly the sort of tree to be expected in a low-lying area next to a river. On the Wicker were the town's archery butts. The Wicker leads to Spital Hill where William de Lovetot had founded a hospital (hence the name 'spital') outside the town in the twelfth century. The northern end of the Wicker is marked by the Grade II listed Wicker Arches, part of a forty-one-arched viaduct built in 1848 to carry the Manchester, Sheffield & Lincolnshire Railway. The viaduct was designed by the architects J. G. Weightman and M. E. Hadfield under the supervision of the railway engineer John Fowler (later Sir John Fowler), the Sheffield-born co-designer of the famous Forth Railway Bridge.

The town's cucking stool was also once in the Wicker before it was moved to Barker's Pool at the other side of the town. Cucking stools were ducking stools for humiliating objectionable persons who spread malicious gossip. They were rather like seesaws but with a seat only at one end. The victim would be locked into the seat, and then would be raised into full public view. The whole contraption would be swivelled round over a river, pond or dam and operators would then duck the culprit a number of times, no doubt shouted and jeered at by a baying crowd.

The Wicker looking towards the Wicker Arches.

Woolley Wood is a very special wood to cherish and enjoy. It is an outstanding example of what woodland historians call an ancient wood. This means that it has been in existence since at least AD 1600. Besides its identification in pre-1600 documents, three characteristics of Woolley Wood point very strongly to it being an ancient wood. First its shape is very uneven, with zig-zags and sinuous bends suggesting that it is what was leftover when land was cleared over a long period of time. This uneven shape is even more marked on early maps before the laying out of Concord Park and the construction of the Ecclesfield Road and the railway. Secondly, Woolley Wood is located on an ancient parish boundary. It is in the ancient parish of Ecclesfield where the parish boundary with Kimberworth (part of the ancient parish of Rotherham) was formed by Blackburn Brook. Surviving ancient woods are often on parish boundaries because by the time woodland was becoming scarce and needed to be protected by our ancestors, woods in the centre of parishes had been cleared. Thirdly it is located on a steep slope.

The name 'Woolley' is an ancient name, spelled in the medieval period as *Wolveleghes* and *Wooleleghes*, and means a 'woodland clearing frequented by wolves'. It is an Old English (Anglo-Saxon) name given to the area sometime between AD 600 and 1100. Wolves were extinct in England by the end of the medieval period.

From at least as early as 1600 until the last years of the nineteenth century, Woolley Wood was managed as a coppice-with-standards. In a coppice-with-standards most of the trees were periodically cut down to the ground, to what is called a stool and from the stool grew multiple stems. The collective name for the multiple coppice poles is underwood. Some of the trees were not coppiced but allowed to grow on to

A wonderful display of bluebells in Woolley Wood.

become mature single-stemmed trees and these were the standards. The coppice produced wood and the standard trees produced timber for building projects. The coppice growth had an amazing number of uses. An important use of coppice poles was for making charcoal, which was the fuel for iron makers until the late eighteenth century and for some steel makers until well into the twentieth century. Hazel rods were used for making hurdles, oak and willow rods were used in basket-making, stout oak poles made good pit props, waterproof alder made excellent clog soles, ash and hazel made good springy brush and tool handles, and even birch brushwood was used to make besom brooms.

What also becomes clear if the wood is visited between April and June is the richness of its ground flora. Many of these woodland flowers are rarely found outside ancient woods. This is because they are slow colonisers, particularly those that spread vegetatively rather than by seed. It is a wonderful bluebell wood with carpets of intense blue stretching for great distances in late April and early May. If you visit the wood at this time of year, please linger and take in fully this wonder of nature. Other widely distributed ancient woodland indicators to look for in Woolley Wood include wood anemone, wild garlic (ramsons), wood sorrel, yellow archangel, yellow pimpernel and the attractive grass wood melick, with its nodding brown seed-heads. The wood is also full of trees that are relatively rare in Sheffield's ancient woods: hornbeam, wild cherry and yew.

Above: A clump of ramsons in the damper part of Woolley Wood.

Right: Wild cherry.
(Illustration by Bob Warburton)

eXtolling the Beauty of Sheffield in the Peak

The idea of creating a national park in the Peak District was born and nurtured in Sheffield. On 7 May 1924 a select gathering of like-minded men and women, disturbed by the increasing defacement of the beauty of the Peak District by 'incongruous and promiscuous development', met at Endcliffe Vale House in the quiet western suburbs of Sheffield. They had come together to discuss the possibility of forming a society for the protection of local scenery. The founder members who were present at the first meeting were a cross-section of Sheffield's leading citizens. The Honorary Secretary elected at the initial meeting was Mrs Ethel Gallimore, widowed during the First World War, who had instigated the meeting. Ethel Gallimore was not only the founder but also the inspiration and prime mover of the new society, which was initially called 'The Sheffield Association for the Protection of Local Scenery'. In 1927 the society became affiliated to the council for the Protection of Rural England and in 1930 became the 'Sheffield and Peak District Branch of the CPRE'. In 1936 a young architect, Gerald Haythornthwaite, joined the branch as secretary and stayed for the next fifty-nine years. He married Ethel Gallimore in 1937. Together, Mr (later Colonel) and Mrs Haythornthwaite masterminded the achievement of the branch's two 'grand purposes': the creation of a Sheffield Green Belt and the designation of the Peak District as a National Park. The Peak District National Park became a reality in 1951 and a third of the total land area of Sheffield (29,640 acres (11,995 hectares)) is in the national park. The most famous quotation about Sheffield – that no one can find the origin of – is that it was 'a dirty picture in a golden frame'. Most of the golden frame lies within those parts of the parish, later the borough and then the city that are included in the Peak District National Park.

The countryside in the Peak Park within Sheffield city boundary is part of the 'Dark Peak' landscape area, an extensive area of semi-natural wilderness. The area is composed of exposed bleak plateaus with dramatic gritstone edges on the highest parts of the Millstone Grit country. Large stretches are covered by heather moorland and blanket bog, without a sign of habitation. These windswept moors contain valuable wildlife habitats in the boggy mires and flashes. Deep narrow valleys carrying fast-flowing river headwaters fringe the area, sometimes heavily wooded on the steep valley sides. Some of these narrow valleys are called cloughs, while others contain in their names the place-name element 'den' meaning a long, narrow, curving valley, as in Ewden (yew-tree valley) and Agden (oak valley). At lower levels on the eastern margins are pastures, mainly for sheep rearing, enclosed by dry stone walls. The larger valleys contain reservoirs, like Broomhead Reservoir in the Ewden valley, which was constructed in 1934. This large reservoir covers 50 hectares and contains more than 1,000 million gallons of water. Seven attractive locations are described below.

The river valleys, reservoirs, the sheep pastures and the open moorland in those parts of Sheffield that lie within the Peak Park are very attractive and heavily used areas for outdoor recreation. At Broomhead Reservoir it is possible to join a fly-fishing and trout-fishing club and members of South Yorkshire Sailing Club can enjoy water sports. But the main activity is walking. For example, a walk of approximately 2.5 miles (4 km) with some uphill sections but not too strenuous, taking around an hour and half, can be taken around Dale Dike Reservoir.

The Redmires Reservoirs lie just within the boundary of the Peak District National Park in the upper Rivelin valley west of the suburb of Fulwood. They lie at an altitude of 1150 ft (352 metres). There are three reservoirs at Redmires: Upper, Middle and Lower. The Middle reservoir was completed in 1836, the Lower reservoir in 1849 and the Upper reservoir in 1854. The reservoirs are fed by streams from the surrounding Hallam Moors, which apart from plantations near the reservoirs consist of unimproved grassland, moorland and blanket bog. The area is popular with walkers and sightseers, and ornithologists can almost always be seen there as the reservoirs form an important breeding ground for waders and wildfowl and a visible migration observation site. In late summer and autumn on the Middle and Upper reservoirs flocks of golden plover and lapwing may be present and large numbers of teal and tufted duck may also be seen. In winter small numbers of goldeneye duck may be observed.

Located in the upper Rivelin valley, Wyming Brook has long held a spell over Sheffielders and it appeared on many Edwardian postcards. From its source at the Redmires reservoirs the brook falls steeply in a north-easterly direction for three-quarters of a mile (just over 1 kilometre) into the lower of the two Rivelin dams. Because of the steep gradient and the rock-strewn stream bed the flow of water can be dramatic as the water dashes down rocky rapids. The valley occupied by Wyming Brook is wooded with a mixture of native broadleaves, mostly birch with some willow carr, and planted larch and pine. The area is a nature reserve managed by Sheffield Wildlife Trust. There is a well-marked footpath beside the brook. There is always a variety of woodland birds to see and hear and from the upper reaches there are wonderful views northwards across the upper Rivelin valley towards Bradfield Moors.

Burbage Edge, a high, vertical, craggy outcrop of gritstone, marks the eastern edge of the Burbage valley in the very south-western corner of Sheffield, abutting on the west and south with the boundary with Derbyshire. The edge is in two distinct parts:

Wyming Brook.

North Edge and South Edge. The edge is popular with climbers because it is sunny and sheltered, there are hundreds of routes up the faces and buttresses and the edge is easily accessible from roads to the north and south. Another appeal is the well-jointed nature of the Millstone Grit rock providing plenty of places for feet and hands.

Carl Wark and Higger Tor both lie in the Burbage valley. They are massive outcrops of Millstone Grit, isolated through faulting and sloping away eastwards. Loose flat boulders lie on the upper surface of the outcrops and others lie at the foot of the outcrops. The separation of these blocks from the outcrop occurred during the last Ice Age when the area lay just outside ice-covered regions in an area of Arctic climate. As the climate ameliorated at the end of the Ice Age, and the ground thawed, many loose blocks simply slid onto lower ground. Because of Carl Wark's shape and steep rocky walls on three sides it was occupied as a fort in Iron Age times. Today because of their altitude (Higger Tor stands at 1254 feet (384 metres)) both of these outcrops make wonderful viewpoints.

Burbage Edge.

Above: Two rock climbers on Burbage Edge.

Below: Higger Tor.

Y

Yarncliffe

Lying right on the boundary of the Peak District National Park to the east of an eastward-facing steep slope lies Yarncliffe House Farm. Yarncliffe is one of those unusual place names that dot the Sheffield landscape and tell us about the natural world that so intrigued our Anglo-Saxon, Viking and medieval ancestors that they named places after them. Yarncliffe is from the Anglo-Saxon *earn cliffe*, meaning a steep edge frequented by eagles. We are sure we do not have to tell our readers that

Yarncliffe.

eagles have been extinct as breeding birds in north Derbyshire and South Yorkshire for hundreds of years. The last recorded breeding pair of golden eagles was in Woodlands Valley, Derwent in north Derbyshire, in 1668. A vagrant bird was seen at Derwent in 1952. Immature White-tailed eagles were seen in the same area in 1920, 1921 and 1939.

It is the same with another bird enshrined in a local place name. One possible meaning of the place name Gleadless, first recorded in 1512, is a 'woodland clearing frequented by kites'. Until recent decades this striking bird of prey was restricted to central Wales through persecution. Reintroduction programmes have now seen it spread into parts of England and Scotland. It was once well established in the wooded parts of the Peak District but had almost completely disappeared by 1880. Since that time only a few red kites have been recorded in north Derbyshire and South Yorkshire. The nearest area to Sheffield where reintroduced birds and their offspring can be observed is on the Harewood estate in northern Leeds where the first birds were released in 1999.

Other interesting local names from birds and animals include Crawshaw (crow wood), Crow Stones, Raven Rocher (raven rocky bank), Brocco Bank (brocco means badger), Woolley Wood (woodland clearing frequented by wolves) and Pismire Hill, *pissemyre* being the Middle English word for an ant. There are also several locations that include or used to include the word 'cockshut' as in the names Cockshutt Farm and Cockshutt Avenue, Drive and Road all in Beauchief, Cockshot Lane in Bolsterstone, Cockshutts Lane in Oughtibridge and Cockshutt Rowe, the old name for Roe Wood. A cockshut or cockshoot was an area in a wood where the game bird, the woodcock, was trapped in nets. And last but not least John Harrison in his 'Exact and Perfect' Survey of Sheffield manor in 1637 recorded a street in the seventeenth century town called Goose Turd Green!

Aerial view of the Gleadless Valley.

Z

Zion Graveyard

This historic graveyard lies beside Zion Lane, a narrow, cobbled thoroughfare running for a short distance parallel to Attercliffe Road, in the aforesaid Attercliffe. Originally the graveyard was located behind the Zion Congregational Church, the site of which had been a place of worship since 1793 and later occupied by a fine-looking place of worship in the Romanesque style with a tower and a spire. As the population of Attercliffe declined in the post-war period, the church became little used and eventually was closed. It became a furniture store that was destroyed by fire in 1987

Mary Anne Rawson's burial place in the Read family grave in Zion Graveyard.

and was eventually demolished. The Zion Sabbath School across the lane from the church still survives and contains a motor-repair business.

The graveyard, located behind the church, survived the radical changes taking place in its vicinity, but became neglected and overgrown. In 2017 the owners, the United Reform Church, put the site up for sale and it seemed it would be destroyed and redeveloped. Not only did it seem that the graves of the families of local industrialists and other local inhabitants who lived and worked in Attercliffe during its boom days would be lost, but also a leading local anti-slavery campaigner, Mary Anne Rawson.

Mary Anne Rawson (1801–87) was the daughter of Joseph Read, who established the Sheffield Smelting Company and lived at Wincobank Hall. She was a founding member of the Sheffield Female Anti-Slavery Society which came into being in 1825 and campaigned for the immediate end of slavery throughout the British Empire. The society campaigned against the use of sugar that had been produced using slave labour in the West Indies. Slavery was abolished in the British West Indies in 1834. In 1837 Rawson became secretary of Sheffield Ladies Association for the Universal Abolition of Slavery.

With the help of the Heritage Lottery Fund the graveyard was purchased by the Friends of Zion Graveyard who intend to manage the site for its heritage value and for its wildlife. They are working with Wildscapes, a subsidiary of Sheffield and Rotherham Wildlife Trust. The Friends will also be conducting research into the family histories of the people buried in the graveyard.

Bibliography

Anon, *Sheffield and Neighbourhood* (Pawson & Brailsford, 1926).

Derry, J., *The Story of Sheffield* (Sir Isaac Pitman & Sons Ltd, 1915).

Gatty, A., *Sheffield Past and Present* (Thomas Rodgers and Bell & Sons Ltd, 1875).

Hey, D., (1998) *A History of Sheffield* (Carnegie Publishing, 1988).

Hunter, J., *Hallamshire: The History and Topography of the Parish of Sheffield* (1819 and revised by A. Gatty, Virtue & Company, 1873).

Jones, M., *The Making of Sheffield* (Wharncliffe Books, 2004).

Jones, M., *Sheffield A History & Celebration* (Francis Frith Collection, 2005).

Jones, M., *Sheffield's Woodland Heritage* (4th edition, Wildtrack Publishing, 2009).

Vickers, J. E., *A Popular History of Sheffield* (EP Publishing Ltd, 1978).

Walton, M., *Sheffield: Its Story and Its Achievements* (The Sheffield Telegraph and Star Limited, 1st edition, 1948).

Acknowledgements

We would like to thank the following for their kind permission in allowing us to take photographs or to use their illustrations or for providing us with background information: Karen Allison of Underbank Chapel, the Reverend Canon Keith Farrow of Sheffield Cathedral, Friends of Manor Lodge, Friends of Meersbrook Park/Heeley Development Trust, Friends of Whinfell Quarry Gardens, Kate Hughes of Green Estate (Sheffield Manor Lodge), Gemma Holden of Sheffield Industrial Museums Trust, Eric Leslie, Peter Machan, Museums Sheffield, Penny Rea (Friends of Zion Graveyard), Holly Roberts of the National Emergency Services Museum, Magda Rogers of the Company of Cutlers in Hallamshire, Sheffield City Archives, Nick Roscoe of Friends of Bishops' House, Sheffield City Council, Sheffield Parks & Countryside Service, Bob Warburton and Allan Womersley. We apologise if we have inadvertently omitted the names of any individual or organisation.

About the Authors

Husband and wife team Melvyn and Joan Jones have co-authored more than twenty books on the local and landscape history of South Yorkshire. These include Amberley titles *Ecclesfield, Chapeltown & High Green Through Time* (2009), *Thorpe Hesley, Scholes and Wentworth Through Time* (2012), *Ecclesfield, Chapeltown & High Green From Old Photographs* (2014) and *Sheffield at Work* (2018).